D1332982

BREAD

✏ LAKELAND

Lakeland and Octopus Publishing Group Limited hereby exclude all liability to the extent permitted by law for any errors or omission in this book and for any loss, damage or expense (whether direct or indirect) suffered by a third party relying on any information contained in this book.

This book was published in 2013 for Lakeland by Hamlyn, a division of Octopus Publishing Group Limited

Endeavour House
189 Shaftesbury Avenue
London WC2H 8JY
United Kingdom
phone +44 (0) 207 632 5400
fax +44 (0) 207 632 5405
www.octopusbooks.co.uk

Printed and bound in China

A catalogue record for this book is available from the British Library.

This publication is copyright. No part of it may be reproduced or transmitted in any form without the written permission of the Publisher.

ISBN 978-0-600-62827-9

© Octopus Publishing Group Limited 2013

The Department of Health advises that eggs should not be consumed raw. This book contains some dishes made with raw or lightly cooked eggs. It is prudent for vulnerable people such as pregnant and nursing mothers, invalids, the elderly, babies and young children to avoid uncooked or lightly cooked dishes made with eggs. Once prepared, these dishes should be kept refrigerated and used promptly.

This book also includes dishes made with nuts and nut derivatives. It is advisable for those with known allergic reactions to nuts and nut derivatives and those who may be potentially vulnerable to these allergies, such as pregnant and nursing mothers, invalids, the elderly, babies and children to avoid dishes made with nuts and nut oils. It is also prudent to check the labels of pre-prepared ingredients for the possible inclusion of nut derivatives.

Some of the recipes in this book have appeared in other publications.

BREAD

Nothing beats the taste and aroma of freshly baked bread. From everyday recipes like Cottage Loaf and Wholemeal Rolls to special-occasion ideas such as Chocolate Brioche and Chilli Corn Bread, this is a mouthwatering collection of 50 recipes for both bread makers and handmade bread.

One of an exciting new series of cookbooks from Lakeland, *Bread* is packed with delicious colour photos and expert hints, tips and techniques for beginners and experienced cooks alike.

These excellent cookbooks are sure to be some of the best loved on your kitchen bookshelf. To discover the rest of the range, together with our unrivalled selection of creative kitchenware, visit one of our friendly Lakeland stores or shop online at www.lakeland.co.uk.

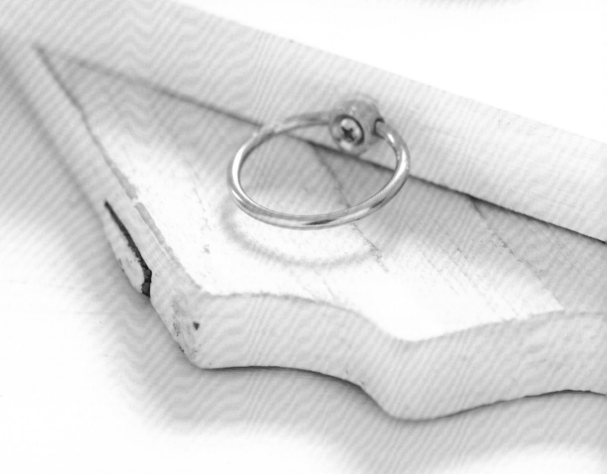

CONTENTS

BASIC INGREDIENTS 6

MAKING BREAD
BY HAND 8

MAKING BREAD IN A
BREAD MAKER 10

SHAPING
TECHNIQUES 12

FINISHING TOUCHES 13

FAMILY FAVOURITES 14

FLAVOURED BREADS 32

SOMETHING SWEET 52

LITTLE BREADS 66

BREAD MAKER BAKING 84

GLOSSARY 124

INDEX 126

CONVERSION CHARTS 128

BASIC INGREDIENTS

The key to successful bread making lies in understanding your ingredients and how they react together. Most of the ingredients used in bread maker baking are the same as those needed for making bread by hand, although for some, such as yeast, you will need to choose one specifically intended for bread makers.

FLOURS

White flour Choose strong white bread flour for well-risen bread with a light, airy texture. This has a higher gluten content for added stretch. Use plain or self-raising flour in yeast-free breads, such as soda bread, only. If you are trying to avoid additives then choose organic, unbleached bread flour.

Wholemeal or wholewheat flour Milled from the whole wheat kernel, this flour contains bran and wheat germ, making it more nutritious and giving the bread a nuttier flavour and coarser

texture. Because bran inhibits the action of gluten, wholemeal loaves take longer to rise. You can compensate for this by mixing half wholemeal bread flour with half strong white bread flour, which will give a lighter texture to the bread.

Brown flour Strong brown bread flour contains only about 80 per cent of the wheat kernel so produces a lighter brown loaf than wholemeal flour. As brown flour contains bran, brown breads rise more slowly.

Granary flour A sweet, nutty flour made with a mixture of wholemeal and white flours with added malted wheat grains, granary flour produces a nutty flavour and a rustic texture. Malthouse flour is similar to granary flour.

Low-gluten flours These include rye, barley and spelt flours. Spelt produces a closer-textured bread but with a good flavour. Barley and rye used on their own produce

a heavier-textured bread so, for lighter results, mix these with strong white bread flour.

Gluten-free flours These are ideal for anyone who has an intolerance to gluten. Bags of mixed gluten-free flours are available from supermarkets. Other gluten-free flours include gram flour (a yellow flour made from chickpeas and also called chickpea flour), quinoa flour, cornmeal flour (made from dried corn kernels, this is used to make American-style yeast-free breads), potato flour, brown rice flour and buckwheat flour, which has a distinctive bitter, earthy taste.

YEAST

The most important ingredient of all, it is available in three types: fresh yeast, traditional dried yeast that requires frothing in water before use, and fast-action dried yeast. Fast-action dried yeast is by far the easiest and most convenient to use and is available in 7g sachets or small packs for mixing directly with the other bread ingredients. Most of the recipes in this book use this type of yeast. It is important that you use precisely the amount of yeast specified in each recipe.

SUGAR

Sugar, which helps activate yeast, can be used in various forms from caster to muscovado or you can use maple syrup, honey, malt extract, treacle or molasses. Don't use artificial sweeteners as the yeast will not react with them properly.

SALT

Salt is an essential ingredient, both as a flavour enhancer and because it controls the rate at which the yeast ferments.

LIQUIDS

This is the main difference between making bread by hand and in a bread maker: the temperature of the water or milk used. Cold water or milk are required for a bread maker, unless you are using a rapid or fast-bake programme, whereas warm liquid must be used when making bread by hand. If the liquid is too hot the yeast will be killed, too cold and the yeast won't be activated. Don't use fresh milk if you are using the time delay programme on your bread maker, as the milk is likely to sour. Use water instead and add a couple of tablespoons of milk powder with the flour, if liked.

ENRICHING INGREDIENTS

Butter, oil, eggs, cream and cheeses can be used to enrich doughs. Butter and oil also act as preservatives and keep bread fresh for longer. Breads made without butter or oil must be eaten on the day they are made. Do not use the timer delay programme on your bread maker if you are using dairy produce or other perishable ingredients.

OTHER FLAVOURINGS

Chopped fresh or dried herbs, crushed or ground spices, dried fruits, nuts and seeds are among the many extra ingredients that can be used to enhance flavour and make even the most basic bread special.

Storing bread

Homemade bread is best eaten fresh on the day it is made, but can be kept fresh for a day or two with the addition of butter or oil. Unlike shop-bought bread, there are no preservatives to increase storage life, but the delicious taste means homemade bread generally gets eaten before it has a chance to go stale.

Leftovers can be wrapped in foil or a plastic bag if the bread has a soft crust, or in a paper bag, fabric bag or bread bin if it is a crusty loaf. Use the following day in sandwiches or for toast. Do not keep bread in the fridge as the cold draws out the moisture, making it dry.

For a longer shelf life, wrap cooled bread in a plastic bag and freeze until required. Or cut the loaf in half and eat half and freeze half. Perhaps the most useful way to freeze bread is in rolls or slices as you can take what you need out of the freezer when you need it.

MAKING BREAD BY HAND

1 Mixing Measure the flour into a large bowl then add the butter and rub it in with the fingertips until the mixture resembles fine breadcrumbs. Stir in the salt, milk powder, if using, sugar and fast-action dried yeast. Make a well in the centre of the flour then, using a wooden spoon, gradually mix in honey, maple syrup or malt extract, if using, and enough warm water to make a soft dough. When the dough begins to form, begin using your hands.

The amount of water given in the recipe is a guide and will vary depending on the type of flour used, the temperature in the kitchen and the level of humidity. Adjust the amount of water as needed and make the dough softer rather than firmer, if you are unsure.

2 Kneading This is essential to mix and activate the dried yeast and to help stretch the gluten in the flour so that the bread can rise fully. Begin by turning the dough out on to lightly floured surface. Stretch the dough by pushing the front half away with the heel of one hand while holding the back of the dough with the other hand. Fold the stretched part of the dough back on itself, give it a quarter turn and repeat for 5 more minutes, until the dough has been turned full circle several times and is a smooth and elastic ball.

3 First rising Dust the mixing bowl with a little extra flour, put the kneaded bread back into the bowl and cover the top loosely with oiled cling film. Leave in a

warm place to rise or 'prove' for about 1 hour or until the dough has doubled in size. This may take more or less time, depending on the temperature in the kitchen.

4 Knocking back Remove the cling film and save for the next rising. Knock back or punch the risen dough in the bowl with your fist to deflate it then pull it out of the bowl. Turn the dough out on to a lightly floured surface and knead well, as before.

5 Shaping Roll the dough back and forth with the palms of your hands in a rocking action until a rope of dough begins to form — about half as long again as the length of the loaf tin. Fold the end of the dough under so that it is an even width and the exact

1a

1b

2

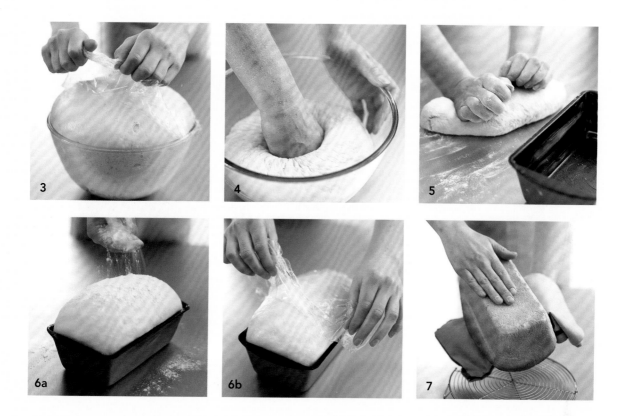

3

4

5

6a

6b

7

length of the tin then lay it in the greased tin. Cover loosely with oiled cling film.

6 Second rising and glazing

Leave the bread in a warm place for 30 minutes for a second and final proving or until the dough rises just above the top of the tin. It is crucial not to over prove the dough at this stage or the bread may collapse in the oven. The dough is ready if when pressed lightly with a fingertip, the dent springs back slowly. If the dent

stays as it is the bread is over proved. Remove the cling film and sprinkle with flour.

7 Baking and testing Bake
bread in a preheated oven, 200°C (400°F), Gas Mark 6, for 25 minutes for a 500g (1lb) loaf, 30 minutes for a large 750g (1½lb) loaf or 35 minutes for an extra large 1kg (2lb) loaf. The bread should be well risen, golden brown and sound hollow when tapped with fingertips. Test the top then loosen the

bread with a palette knife, holding the tin with oven gloves. Turn out on to a wire rack and tap the base of the bread to double check it is done. If the base feels a little soft, return it to the oven and place directly on to the oven shelf. Check again after 5 minutes and, if done transfer to wire rack to cool.

Tip Always leave hot bread to cool for at least 30 minutes before slicing.

MAKING BREAD IN A BREAD MAKER

Check your manual
Not all bread makers are the same so always check your manual or cookbook before trying a recipe for the first time. Alter the amounts of yeast or other ingredients following manufacturer's directions, if necessary. You may also need to add the ingredients in the order that the manufacturers specify if different to the steps shown in this book.

Read the bread maker manual first so you are familiar with the settings and how to operate them. The many menu options available for programme, loaf and crust colour may seem a little daunting at first, but will quickly become second nature.

1 Before you begin Stand the bread maker on the work surface ensuring there is plenty of space around it for ventilation and that it is out of direct sunlight and draughts, if possible. With the bread maker unplugged, pull the bread tin (bucket) upwards and out of the maker, giving it a little twist if necessary, depending on your maker.

2 Preparing the maker Insert the paddle or kneader blade on to the spindle in the base of the tin and check that it is secure and turns easily. When your bread maker has been used a number of times, double check that there are no baked-on pieces of bread on the spindle before fitting the blade, otherwise it will not be able to rotate at the correct speed.

3 Adding wet ingredients Add the wet ingredients to the tin. Pour in the cold water or milk (unless setting to a rapid/fastbake programme where warm water is required). Beat the eggs before adding them, and then add either melted butter or butter softened to room temperature so that it mixes into the flour easily. Honey is best added at this stage too. (Do not add perishable ingredients if using the delay timer facility.)

4 Adding dry ingredients Spoon the flour over the liquid, making sure the flour covers the liquid completely, then add the dried milk powder, if using, salt, sugar, dried herbs or spices to different corners of the tin. Make a slight dip into the centre of the flour making sure that the yeast will not come into contact with the liquid. This is especially important if you are using the delay timer facility. Measure the yeast carefully and sprinkle it into the dip.

5 Inserting the tin into the maker Insert the tin into the bread maker carefully, lining up any arrows on the tin with any in the bread maker and making sure the tin is clicked into place securely. Shut the lid.

6 Selecting the programme Plug in the bread maker and select the programme required for the type and size of loaf being made. Some makers may also have a selection for pale, medium and dark crust too. Use the setting suggested in the recipes later on in this book, referring to your manual and adapting as necessary.

7 Starting the programme Press start. Some makers may operate a warming period while others will warm and mix immediately. Obviously those makers that mix and warm simultaneously will have shorter programme times.

8 Using the raisin beep Towards the end of the mixing stage a beep, known as the raisin beep, will sound on your maker. At this point, you can add flavourings such as dried fruit, sun-dried tomatoes or spring onions before allowing the programme to continue. Double check it after 10 minutes to make sure that the added ingredients have been fully incorporated into the dough. If not, scrape any unmixed additions down the side of tin with a plastic spatula, making sure to keep the spatula out of the way of the blade.

9 The end of the programme Close the lid and allow the programme to continue. When it has finished, another beep will sound. Take out risen dough, for baked bread hold the tin handles. The bread can be removed at this stage by holding the tin handles with oven gloves and simply lifting it out of the maker. Alternatively, the bread may be left in the maker

and will keep hot for up to 90 minutes, depending on the length of the programme. Don't forget that the maker will be hot when you open the lid so try not to lean over it wearing glasses or contact lenses as they may steam up.

10 Removing the bread Holding the tin sides with oven gloves, loosen the bread from the tin with a plastic spatula or turn the tin upside down and shake several times. Once loosened, turn the bread out on to a wire rack and leave it to cool for at least 30 minutes to allow the steam to escape. The paddle or kneader blade should stay in the tin. If not, check the base of the bread and remove it carefully, remembering that it will be hot. Turn the maker off at the plug and leave it to cool.

Tip Check on the dough's progress from time to time. If you find pockets of dry ingredients around the sides of the tin, scrape them down with a plastic spatula, making sure that the spatula does not get in the way of the kneader blade. Adjust the consistency of the dough by adding a tablespoon or two of extra liquid, if it seems a little dry or a tablespoon or two of extra flour, if it looks sticky.

8

9

SHAPING TECHNIQUES

ADDING HOLES

For loaves, such as a Couronne (see page 24), make a small hole in the centre with a fingertip then gradually enlarge it by rolling the dough around a well floured fist.

Keeping bread dough

If you suddenly get interrupted and don't have time to shape and bake the bread dough as planned, then it can be stored for several hours or overnight in the fridge, tightly covered with oiled cling film. Knock the dough back once or twice if it gets very big. Allow the dough to come to room temperature then knead it well, shape and then leave for a final rising in a warm place until it is half as big again. Bake as the recipe.

PRETZELS

1 Make a long thin rope of dough then curve in a wide arc. Taking the ends of the rope in separate hands, twist the dough together about half way down the length.

2 Press the ends of the rope on to the sides of the loop to give the traditional knotted effect (see Salted Pretzels, page 109).

CUTTING DOUGH

1 Make criss-cross lines over a floured loaf, before proving, using a sharp knife (see Fig & Walnut Bread, page 54).

2 Slash the top of a just-risen loaf along it's length with a sharp knife or a new craft knife. It not only makes the bread look more interesting, but helps to speed up cooking.

FINISHING TOUCHES

GARNISHES & DECORATIONS

Sprinkling the top of a shaped loaf or roll not only looks attractive but also gives an indication of whether the bread is sweet or savoury.

Savoury toppings: a little flour, barley flakes, porridge oats, cornmeal, wheat germ, linseeds, caraway, fennel, sunflower, sesame, pumpkin or poppy seeds, coarse salt flakes, paprika, dried chilli flakes, mustard seeds, grated cheese, fresh herbs, sliced tomatoes. Be wary of using sun-dried tomatoes unless stored in oil as these scorch during baking.

Sweet toppings: white or coloured sugars, icing sugar, roughly crushed sugar lumps, brown coffee crystals, strips of citron peel, roughly chopped nuts, dried fruits, grated or chopped chocolate or cocoa.

GLAZES & FINISHES

Brushing a glaze over the shaped dough just before baking enhances the colour and sheen of the bread and adds extra flavour to the crust.

Egg yolk and water: mix 1 egg yolk with 1 tablespoon cold water and brush over risen dough for a shiny glaze. Whole egg tends to go streaky during cooking.

Egg white and water: mix 1 egg white with 1 tablespoon cold water for a paler crust with a softer sheen.

Melted butter: can be brushed over bread before and after baking to darken the crust as it cooks and to help keep the baked crust soft.

Olive oil: can be drizzled over a flat Mediterranean bread just as it goes into the oven and again for a soft glistening finish as it comes out. Choose virgin olive oil for a stronger, more intense flavour.

Salted water: mix 3 teaspoons salt with 3 tablespoons water and brush over risen dough just before baking for a crisp crust. For a less salty glaze, add 1 teaspoon caster sugar, if liked.

Milk wash: brush milk over white risen dough for a soft crust and as a 'glue' for sticking grains and seeds on to the top of breads

Milk and sugar glaze: dissolve 2 tablespoons caster sugar in 4 tablespoons milk and boil for 1 minute. Brush over just-baked sweet breads, malt breads and hot cross buns for a glossy finish.

Preserves: warm 3 tablespoons marmalade or apricot jam with 1–2 tablespoons water, orange juice, brandy or liqueur for a sticky glaze to apply after baking to sweet breads.

Honey or golden syrup: warm a little in the microwave or a small pan and then brush over the top of a just-baked loaf or rolls for a very sticky but highly glossy glaze.

Glacé icing: mix 125g sifted icing sugar with 4–5 teaspoons fresh lemon or orange juice or water to make a thin-coating icing and drizzle from a spoon or brush over hot or cold sweet loaves or rolls.

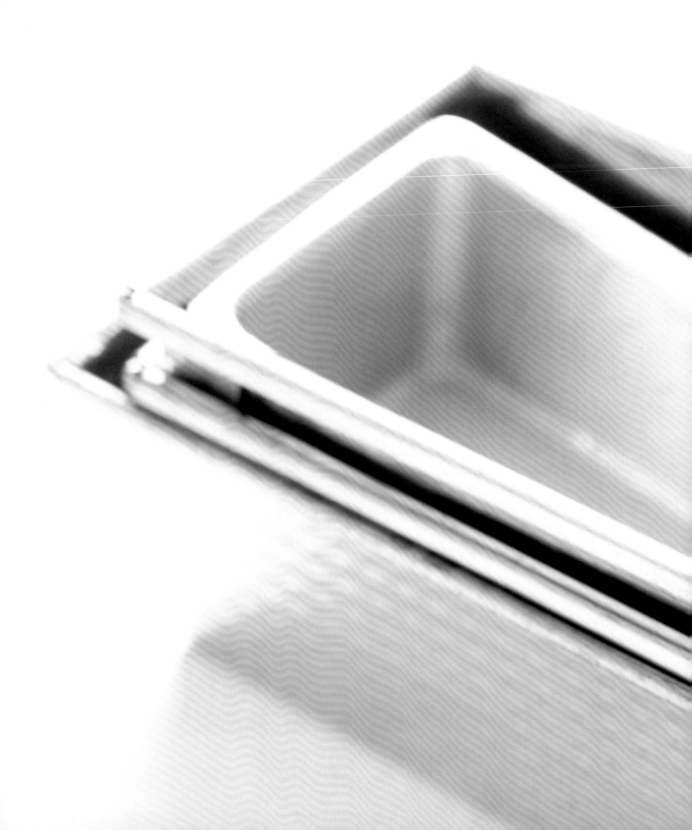

FAMILY FAVOURITES

COTTAGE LOAF

750g strong white bread flour, sifted
7g sachet fast-action dried yeast
2 teaspoons salt
1 teaspoon caster sugar
15g chilled butter, diced
450ml warm water

1 Combine the flour, yeast, salt and sugar in a bowl. Rub in the butter. Add the water and bring the ingredients together to form a soft dough. Knead on a lightly floured surface for 8–10 minutes until smooth and elastic.

2 Shape into a ball and put the dough back into the bowl, cover loosely with oiled cling film and leave in a warm place to rise for 1 hour or until doubled in size.

3 On a lightly floured surface, knock back the dough, shape into an oval and press, seam side down in an greased 1kg (2lb) loaf tin. Cover with oiled cling film and leave to rise for 30 minutes more until dough reaches the top of the tin.

4 Bake in a preheated oven, 230°C (450°F), Gas Mark 8, for 15 minutes. Reduce oven to 200°C (400°F), Gas Mark 6, and bake for 15 minutes more until risen and hollow sounding when tapped underneath. Transfer to a wire rack to cool.

prep + cook time 40 minutes + kneading, proving and shaping time
makes 1 large loaf

WHEAT GERM & HONEY BREAD

475g strong white bread flour
50g wheat germ
1 teaspoon salt
2 tablespoons butter
1¼ teaspoons fast-action dried
  yeast
2 teaspoons clear honey
275ml water
1 egg yolk, to glaze
2 tablespoons sesame seeds

1 Put the flour, wheat germ and salt into a large bowl. Add the butter and rub in with the fingertips until the mixture resembles fine breadcrumbs. Stir in the yeast, then add the honey and gradually mix in enough warm water to make a soft dough.
2 Knead well on a lightly floured surface for 5 minutes until the dough is smooth and elastic. Put the dough back into the bowl, cover loosely with oiled cling film and leave in a warm place to rise for 1 hour or until doubled in size.
3 Tip the dough out on to a lightly floured surface and knead well. Shape into a large oval about 23cm long then transfer to a greased baking sheet and make slashes along the top at 2.5cm intervals with a sharp knife.
4 Cover loosely with oiled cling film and leave to rise for 30 minutes or until half as big again.

5 Brush with the egg yolk mixed with 1 tablespoon of water and bake in a preheated oven, 200°C (400°F), Gas Mark 6, for 10 minutes. Brush with egg again then sprinkle with the sesame seeds. Bake for 15–20 minutes more until the bread is deep golden brown and sounds hollow when tapped with the fingertips. Check after 10 minutes and cover with foil if overbrowning.
6 Transfer to a wire rack to cool.

prep + cook time 45-50 minutes + kneading, proving and shaping time
makes 1 large loaf

MIXED SEED BREAD

475g malthouse bread flour
2 tablespoons butter
1 tablespoon brown sugar
1½ teaspoons salt
3 tablespoons sesame seeds
3 tablespoons sunflower seeds
3 tablespoons linseeds
1¼ teaspoons fast-action dried
   yeast
300ml water
milk, to glaze
extra seeds, optional

1 Put the flour into a large bowl, add the butter and rub in with the fingertips until the mixture resembles fine breadcrumbs. Stir in the sugar, salt, seeds and yeast. Gradually mix in enough warm water to make a soft dough.

2 Knead well on a lightly floured surface for 5 minutes until the dough is smooth and elastic. Put back into the bowl, cover loosely with oiled cling film and leave in a warm place to rise for 1 hour or until doubled in size.

3 Turn out on to a lightly floured surface and knead again for 5 minutes. Put the dough into a greased 20cm round loose-bottomed tin.

4 Cover loosely with oiled cling film and leave in a warm place to rise for 30 minutes or until the dough reaches the top of the tin.

5 Remove the cling film, brush the top with a little milk and sprinkle with some extra seeds, if liked. Bake in a preheated oven, 200°C (400°F), Gas Mark 6, for 30–35 minutes or until the bread is well risen, golden and sounds hollow when tapped. Cover with foil after 15 minutes to prevent overbrowning.

6 Transfer to a wire rack to cool.

prep + cook time 40–45 minutes + kneading and proving time
makes 1 large loaf

FARMHOUSE WHITE LOAF

300g strong white bread flour
1 tablespoon butter
1 teaspoon granulated sugar
½ teaspoon salt
1 teaspoon fast-action dried yeast
175ml warm water

1 Put the flour into a large bowl, add the butter and rub in with the fingertips until the mixture resembles fine breadcrumbs. Stir in the sugar, salt and yeast. Gradually mix in enough warm water to make a soft dough.

2 Knead well on a lightly floured surface for 5 minutes until the dough is smooth and elastic. Put the dough back into the bowl, cover loosely with oiled cling film and leave in a warm place to rise for 45 minutes or until doubled in size.

3 Tip the dough out on to a lightly floured surface, knead well then put into a greased 500g (1lb) loaf tin.

4 Cover loosely with oiled cling film and leave in a warm place to rise for 30 minutes or until the dough reaches the top of the tin.

5 Remove the cling film, sprinkle with flour and bake in a preheated oven, 200°C (400°F), Gas Mark 6, for 25 minutes, covering with foil after 20 minutes to prevent overbrowning.

6 Transfer to a wire rack to cool.

prep + cook time 35 minutes + kneading and proving time
makes 1 small loaf
tip For a richer, golden crust add 2 teaspoons of milk powder

COURONNE

500g unbleached strong white
 bread flour
1½ teaspoons salt
2 teaspoons caster sugar
1¼ teaspoons fast-action dried
 yeast
200g natural yogurt
175ml warm water

1 Put the flour into a large bowl then stir in the salt, sugar and yeast. Add the yogurt then gradually mix in enough warm water to make a soft dough.

2 Knead on a lightly floured surface for 5 minutes or until the dough is smooth and elastic. Put it back into the bowl, cover loosely with oiled cling film and leave to rise in a warm place for 1 hour or until it has doubled in size.

3 Tip the dough out on to a lightly floured surface and knead well. Shape into a round then make a small hole in the centre with the fingertips, enlarge with a fist (see page 12) until the hole is about 12cm wide and the bread is a ring of about 20cm in diameter.

4 Transfer to a greased baking sheet and mark with 3 or 4 cuts if liked. Grease the base of a small basin and place in the centre of the bread to keep the 'hole' intact. Cover the bread and basin loosely with oiled cling film and leave it in a warm place for 30 minutes or until it is half as big again.

5 Remove the cling film and basin, sprinkle the dough with flour and bake in a preheated oven, 220°C (420°F), Gas Mark 7, for 20–25 minutes until it is well risen and browned and the bread sounds hollow when tapped with the fingertips. Cover with foil after 15 minutes if overbrowning.

6 Transfer to a wire rack to cool.

prep + cook time 30–35 minutes + kneading, proving and shaping time
makes 1 loaf

BUTTERED GARLIC & BASIL STICKS

400g strong white bread flour
1 teaspoon salt
1 teaspoon caster sugar
1¼ teaspoons fast-action dried
  yeast
2 tablespoons olive oil
200ml warm water
coarse sea salt

to finish
100g butter
4 garlic cloves, finely chopped
1 small bunch fresh basil
black pepper

1 Put the flour into a large bowl then stir in the salt, sugar and yeast. Add the olive oil then gradually mix in enough warm water to make a soft dough.
2 Knead well on a lightly floured surface for 5 minutes until the dough is smooth and elastic. Put the dough back into the bowl, cover loosely with oiled cling film and leave in a warm place to rise for 1 hour or until doubled in size.
3 Tip the dough out on to a lightly floured surface, knead well then cut in half. Roll each half out to a thin oval about 35 x 18cm. Transfer to 2 greased baking sheets and cut into 2.5cm strips, making cuts a little in from the edge of the dough so that strips are still held together at the ends within the oval shape.
4 Sprinkle the dough with a little coarse salt. Cover loosely with oiled cling film and leave in a warm place for 30 minutes until the bread has risen around the edges.

5 Remove the cling film and bake in a preheated oven, 220°C (425°F), Gas Mark 7, for 8–10 minutes until the bread is golden and sounds hollow when tapped with the fingertips. Transfer to 2 large plates.
6 Melt a small piece of butter in a saucepan and add the garlic. Fry for 2–3 minutes until just beginning to brown. Add the remaining butter, basil leaves torn into pieces and black pepper to taste. When the butter has melted, brush this over the hot bread, separate into sticks and serve immediately.

prep + cook time 25 minutes + kneading, proving and shaping time
makes about 20 sticks
tip To make these breadsticks in advance, brush the hot breads thinly with a little of the butter mixture, then leave to cool completely on a wire rack. Warm them when needed and brush with the remaining warmed butter when ready to serve.

ROSEMARY & OLIVE OIL FOCACCIA

500g strong white bread flour
7g sachet fast-action dried yeast
1 tablespoon chopped fresh
 rosemary, plus extra for
 sprinkling
1 tablespoon sea salt, plus extra
 for sprinkling
275ml warm water
2 tablespoons extra virgin olive
 oil, plus extra for drizzling

1 Combine the flour, yeast, rosemary and salt in a bowl. Add the water and oil and bring the ingredients together to form a soft dough. Shape into a ball and transfer to a lightly floured surface. Knead for 8–10 minutes until the dough is smooth and elastic.
2 Shape into a ball, put the dough back into the bowl, cover loosely with oiled cling film and leave in a warm place to rise for 1 hour or until doubled in size.
3 Knock back the dough on a lightly floured surface and roll out to form a round. Press the dough into a 25cm ovenproof frying pan or cake tin. Cover with oiled cling film and leave to rise for 1 hour.
4 Using your fingers press indentations over the dough. Cover with oiled cling film and leave to prove for a final 30 minutes until well risen.
5 Sprinkle the dough with a little salt, drizzle with a little oil and scatter over some rosemary. Bake in a preheated oven, 200°C (400°F), Gas Mark 6, for about 25 minutes until risen and golden. Transfer to a wire rack to cool and serve while still warm.

prep + cook time 35 minutes + kneading, proving and shaping time
makes 1 large loaf

PITTA BREAD

375g strong white bread flour
1 teaspoon salt
1 teaspoon caster sugar
1½ teaspoons fast-action dried
  yeast
1 tablespoon olive oil
250ml warm water

1 Put the flour into a large bowl then stir in the salt, sugar and yeast. Add the oil then gradually mix in enough warm water to make a soft dough.

2 Knead well on a lightly floured surface for 5 minutes until the dough is smooth and elastic. Put the dough back into the bowl, cover loosely with oiled cling film and leave in a warm place to rise for 1 hour or until doubled in size.

3 Tip the dough out on to a lightly floured surface, knead well then cut into 8 pieces. Roll out the pieces into ovals of about 15 cm or into ovals a little smaller than your hand.

4 Put the dough on to pieces of oiled cling film and cover loosely with more oiled cling film. Leave to rise for 15 minutes.

5 Heat 3 baking sheets in a preheated oven, 220°C (425°F), Gas Mark 7, for 5–7 minutes. Rinse the trays with cold water so that the breads won't stick then quickly put the breads on the hot baking trays and cook for 6–8 minutes until puffy and just beginning to brown.

6 Serve the pitta breads warm or wrap them in a clean tea towel to keep them soft and leave to cool on a wire rack. To serve, slit open and stuff the pockets with fillings.

prep + cook time about 15 minutes + kneading, proving and shaping time
makes 8
tip To reheat the breads, sprinkle with a little water and cook under a hot grill for 1 minute on each side.

FLAVOURED BREADS

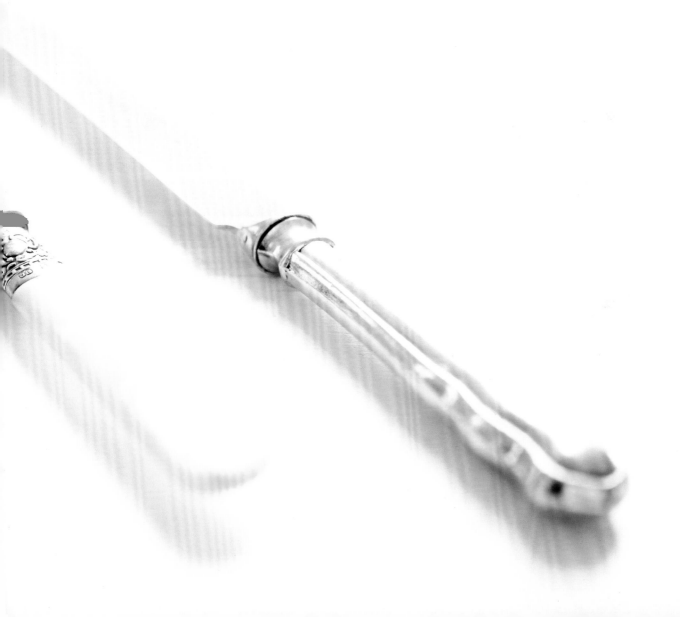

OLIVE BREAD

550g strong white bread flour
1½ teaspoons fast-action dried
  yeast
2½ teaspoons sea salt
250ml warm water
50ml extra virgin olive oil
125g pitted black olives, roughly
  chopped

1 Sift 500g of the flour into a large bowl and stir in the yeast and salt. Add the water and oil and bring the ingredients together to form a soft dough. Knead for 8–10 minutes on a lightly floured surface until the dough is smooth and elastic.

2 Turn out the dough on to a lightly floured surface, add the olives and the rest of the flour and knead into the dough. Shape into a ball and put the dough back into the bowl, cover loosely with oiled cling film and leave in a warm place to rise for 1 hour or until doubled in size.

3 Turn out the dough on to a lightly floured surface and knock out the trapped air. Shape the dough into a log and then roll it out to form a thin sausage about 60 cm long. Form the sausage into a ring, pressing the ends together, and transfer it to a large, lightly greased baking sheet. Cover it loosely with oiled cling film and leave to rise for a further 30 minutes.

4 Bake in a preheated oven, 220°C (425°F), Gas Mark 7, for 25 minutes until the bread is risen and sounds hollow when it is tapped underneath. Transfer to a wire rack to cool.

prep + cook time 40 minutes + kneading, proving and shaping time
makes 1 large loaf
tip To make rolls, divide the dough into 8 pieces and bake for 18–20 minutes until golden.

SAGE & PARMESAN FLUTES

500g malthouse bread flour
65g Parmesan cheese, grated
3 tablespoons fresh chopped
 sage or 2 teaspoons dried
1½ teaspoons salt
1½ teaspoons fast-action dried
 yeast
3 tablespoons olive oil
1 tablespoon honey
300ml warm water
extra flour or Parmesan, for
 dusting

1 Put the flour into a large bowl. Stir in the cheese, sage, salt and yeast. Add the oil and honey, then gradually mix in enough warm water to make a smooth soft dough.

2 Knead well on a lightly floured surface for 5 minutes until the dough is smooth and elastic. Put it back into the bowl, cover loosely with oiled cling film and leave the dough to rise in a warm place for 1 hour or until doubled in size.

3 Tip the dough out on to a lightly floured surface, knead well then cut into 3 equal-sized pieces. Roll each piece into a 30cm length and then transfer it to a large greased baking sheet. Leave enough space between the loaves to allow them to rise.

4 Make diagonal cuts along the top of each loaf, at intervals. Cover loosely with oiled cling film and leave in a warm place for 30 minutes until well risen.

5 Sprinkle the loaves with a little extra flour or Parmesan and bake in a preheated oven, 200°C (400°F), Gas Mark 6, for 15 minutes until well risen and golden and the

bread sounds hollow when tapped with the fingertips.

6 Transfer to a wire rack to cool.

prep + cook time 25 minutes + kneading, proving and shaping time
makes 3 loaves
tip In place of sage, try fresh basil, marjoram or chopped chives, or dried herbes de Provence.

GLUTEN-FREE FETA & HERB LOAF

200g polenta
100g rice flour
50g milk powder
pinch of salt
7g sachet fast-action dried yeast
2 teaspoons caster sugar
2 teaspoons xanthan gum
3 eggs, beaten
2 tablespoons chopped fresh
   herbs
450ml warm water
100g feta cheese, crumbled

1 Sift together the polenta, flour, milk powder and salt in a large bowl and stir well to combine. Stir in the yeast, sugar and xanthan gum.

2 Mix together the eggs, herbs and warm water in a separate bowl, add to the dry ingredients and combine to form a smooth mixture. Beat for 5 minutes, then stir in the feta.

3 Spoon the mixture in a greased 1kg (2lb) loaf tin, cover with oiled cling film and leave in warm place to rise for about 30 minutes until the mixture is near the top of the tin.

4 Place in a preheated oven, 180°C (350°F), Gas Mark 4, for about 45 minutes or until the loaf is brown and sounds hollow when tapped on the bottom. Transfer to a wire rack to cool.

prep + cook time 55 minutes + proving time
makes 1 large loaf

GRANARY & PUMPKIN BREAD

475g granary bread flour
2 tablespoons butter
1½ teaspoons salt
50g pumpkin seeds
1¼ teaspoons fast-action dried
   yeast
¼ plain or orange flavoured
   1000mg Vitamin C tablet
2 tablespoons malt extract
300ml warm water

to finish
milk, to glaze
pumpkin seeds

1 Put the flour into a large bowl, add the butter and rub in with the fingertips until the mixture resembles fine breadcrumbs. Stir in the salt, pumpkin seeds and yeast. Crush the vitamin C tablet between 2 teaspoons and add to the bowl with the malt extract. Gradually mix in enough warm water to make a soft dough.
2 Tip the dough out on to a lightly floured surface and knead for 5 minutes until it is smooth and elastic. Put it back into the bowl, cover loosely with oiled cling film and leave in a warm place for 1 hour or until it has doubled in size.
3 Tip the dough out on to a lightly floured surface, knead well then roll out and press into the base of a greased 1kg (2lb) loaf tin. Cover loosely with oiled cling film and leave to rise for 30 minutes or until the dough is just above the top of the tin.

4 Remove the cling film, brush the dough with milk and sprinkle with extra pumpkin seeds. Bake in a preheated oven, 200°C (400°F), Gas Mark 6, for 25–30 minutes, covering with foil after 15 minutes to prevent overbrowning.
5 Transfer to a wire rack to cool.

prep + cook time 35–40 minutes
+ kneading and proving time
makes 1 large loaf

OLIVE & TOMATO TEAR & SHARE BREAD

475g strong white bread flour
1 teaspoon salt
1 teaspoon caster sugar
1¼ teaspoons fast-action dried yeast
2 tablespoons olive oil
275ml warm water
125g pitted or stuffed green olives, roughly chopped
40g sun-dried tomatoes (not in oil), roughly chopped
coarse sea salt and paprika, to garnish

1 Put the flour, salt, sugar and yeast into a large bowl. Add the olive oil then gradually mix in enough warm water to make a soft dough.

2 Knead well on a lightly floured surface for 5 minutes until the dough is smooth and elastic. Put the dough back into the bowl, cover loosely with oiled cling film and leave in a warm place to rise for 1 hour or until doubled in size.

3 Tip the dough out on to a lightly floured surface and knead well. Gradually work in the chopped olives and tomatoes. Pat into a rough circle about 20 cm in diameter. Transfer to a greased baking sheet and mark the dough into 8 wedges, but do not cut right through to the base.

4 Sprinkle with the salt and paprika then cover loosely with oiled cling film and leave in a warm place to rise for 30 minutes or until half as big again.

5 Remove the cling film and bake in a preheated oven, 200°C (400°F), Gas Mark 6, for 30 minutes. Check after 15 minutes and cover with foil if overbrowning.

6 Transfer to a wire rack to cool.

prep + cook time 40 minutes + kneading, proving and shaping time
makes 1 large loaf
tip The sun-dried tomatoes in this recipe are those that come packed in a cellophane bag. If you wish to use the kind preserved in oil, drain well and use double the quantity as the oil that has soaked into them makes them heavier.

SPICED POTATO & ONION BREAD

200g potato, peeled
1 tablespoon sunflower oil
150g onion, finely chopped
1½ teaspoons cumin seeds,
 roughly crushed
1½ teaspoons fennel seeds,
 roughly crushed
½ teaspoon turmeric
½ teaspoon paprika
2 tablespoons butter
475g strong white bread flour
2 teaspoons caster sugar
2 teaspoons salt
1½ teaspoons fast-action dried
 yeast
200ml warm water
melted butter, to finish

1 Halve the potato then cook it in a small saucepan of boiling water for 15 minutes or until tender. Meanwhile, heat the oil in a frying pan, add the onion and fry gently until softened and pale golden. Stir in the spices and cook for 1 minute.
2 Drain the potato and mash finely with the butter. Leave to cool slightly.
3 Put the flour into a large bowl then stir in the sugar, salt and yeast. Add the potato, and all but 2 tablespoons of the spiced onions. Mix in enough warm water to make a soft dough.
4 Knead well on a lightly floured surface for 5 minutes until the dough is smooth and elastic. Put the dough back into the bowl, cover loosely with oiled cling film and leave in a warm place to rise for 1 hour or until doubled in size.
5 Tip the dough out on to a lightly floured surface, knead well then press into a greased 20cm springform tin, mark into wedges and sprinkle with the reserved onions. Cover loosely with oiled cling film and leave for 30 minutes or until the dough reaches the top of the tin.

6 Remove the cling film and bake in a preheated oven, 200°C (400°F), Gas Mark 6, for 30–35 minutes until the bread is golden and sounds hollow when tapped with the fingertips.
7 Transfer to a wire rack and brush with a little extra melted butter.

prep + cook time about 1 hour + kneading and proving time
makes 1 large loaf

CHILLI CORN BREAD

1 tablespoon caster sugar
150g yellow cornmeal
250g plain flour
3 teaspoons baking powder
1 teaspoon bicarbonate of soda
1 teaspoon salt
black pepper
50g butter, softened
50g Parmesan cheese, grated
2 large whole dried chillies, finely
   chopped
6 spring onions, finely chopped
2 eggs, beaten
150g natural yogurt
300ml milk

1 Line the base and grease the base and sides of a deep 18 cm square cake tin.
2 Put the dry ingredients into a large bowl, add the butter, cheese, chillies and onion. Whisk the eggs, yogurt and milk together in a jug and add to the dry ingredients and mix well. Spoon the mixture into the prepared cake tin and level the surface.
3 Bake in a preheated oven, 160°C (325°F), Gas Mark 3, for 45–55 minutes or until well risen and golden and the top has cracked slightly. Check the bread is cooked by inserting a skewer into the centre. If it comes out cleanly, the bread is ready.
4 Transfer to a wire rack and peel off the lining paper. Leave to cool.

prep + cook time about 1 hour 10 minutes
makes 1 large loaf

ROASTED RED PEPPER & ROSEMARY SLIPPERS

200g strong white bread flour
250g granary bread flour
1 tablespoon finely chopped
  rosemary
1½ teaspoons salt
1 teaspoon caster sugar
1¼ teaspoons fast-action dried
  yeast
2 tablespoons olive oil
250ml warm water

filling
2 red peppers
1 yellow pepper
2 tablespoons olive oil
4 teaspoons balsamic vinegar
1 tablespoon sun-dried tomato
  paste
salt and black pepper

to finish
2 tablespoons olive oil
fresh rosemary leaves

1 Put the flours into a large bowl then stir in the rosemary, salt, sugar and yeast. Add the oil and gradually mix in enough warm water to make a soft dough.
2 Knead well on a lightly floured surface for 5 minutes until the dough is smooth and elastic. Put back into the bowl, cover loosely with oiled cling film and leave in a warm place for 1 hour or until doubled in size.
3 Meanwhile, cut the peppers into quarters, removing the cores and seeds. Arrange on a grill rack with the skins uppermost and drizzle with the oil. Place under a preheated grill for 10 minutes until the skins are blackened. Wrap them in foil and leave to cool.
4 Remove the pepper skins with a small knife, then cut into thin strips. Season and toss with the vinegar.
5 Tip the dough out on to a lightly floured surface, knead well then cut in two. Roll each piece to a thin oval about 28 x 15cm. Spread with the tomato paste. Spoon half the peppers down the centre of each oval, then fold the dough in half lengthways to cover the mixture.

6 Carefully lift each loaf on to a large greased baking sheet. Sprinkle the tops with the remaining peppers then cover loosely with oiled cling film. Leave in a warm place for 30 minutes until well risen.
7 Remove the cling film and drizzle with oil and sprinkle with the extra rosemary. Bake in a preheated oven, 220°C (425°F), Gas Mark 7, for 15 minutes. Cover with foil if overbrowning. Serve hot or cold.

prep + cook time 25 minutes
+ kneading, proving and shaping time
makes 2 loaves
tip If you plan to reheat this bread, slightly undercook it at first so it doesn't dry out when it is reheated.

BACON & BEER SODA BREAD

125g smoked bacon, finely
  chopped
350g wholemeal bread flour
125g medium oatmeal
2 teaspoons baking powder
1½ teaspoons bicarbonate of
  soda
1 teaspoon salt
300ml light beer
2 tablespoons vegetable oil

1 Dry-fry the bacon for 3–4 minutes until golden. Set aside to cool. Combine the dry ingredients in a bowl, add the beer, oil and cooled bacon and work the ingredients together to form a soft dough. Transfer to a lightly floured surface and knead the dough for 2–3 minutes until it is smooth.

2 Shape the dough into a flat round, about 18 cm across, and transfer it to a lightly floured baking sheet. Use a sharp knife to score into 8 wedges, cutting down about 1 cm into the dough.

3 Bake in a preheated oven, 220°C (425°F), Gas Mark 7, for 15 minutes. Reduce the temperature to 190°C (375°F), Gas Mark 5, and bake for a further 20–25 minutes until the bread sounds hollow when tapped lightly underneath. Transfer to a wire rack to cool.

prep + cook time 45–50 minutes + kneading, proving and shaping time
preparation time 30 minutes
makes 1 small loaf

SOMETHING SWEET

FIG & WALNUT BREAD

450g strong white bread flour, sifted
250g wholemeal bread flour
7g sachet fast-action dried yeast
2 teaspoons salt
400ml warm water
1 tablespoon molasses
125g walnuts, toasted and chopped
125g dried figs, finely chopped

1 Put the flours in a large bowl and stir in the yeast and salt. Add the water and molasses and bring together to form a soft dough. Knead for 8–10 minutes until the dough is smooth and elastic. Add the walnuts and figs and knead for a further 2 minutes until evenly incorporated.

2 Shape the dough into a ball and put it back in the bowl. Cover loosely with oiled cling film and leave in a warm place to rise for 1–1½ hours or until doubled in size.

3 Turn out the dough and knock out the air. Divide the dough in half and form each piece into a small, slightly flattened round.

4 Put the rounds on a large, floured baking sheet, cover loosely with oiled cling film and leave to rise for a further 30–45 minutes until they have doubled in size.

5 Use a sharp knife to cut a diamond pattern into each round (see page 12) and bake in a preheated oven, 220°C (425°F), Gas Mark 7, for 30–35 minutes until the bread has risen and sounds hollow when tapped underneath. Transfer to a wire rack to cool.

prep + cook time 40–45 minutes + kneading, proving and shaping time
makes 2 round loaves

DATE & WALNUT SODA BREAD

200g strong wholemeal bread
   flour
275g plain flour
1 teaspoon bicarbonate of soda
½ teaspoon salt
125g soft light brown sugar
250ml milk
1 teaspoon cream of tartar
50g butter, melted
1 egg, beaten
75g walnut pieces
175g pitted dates, chopped
extra flour, for sprinkling

1 Put the flours, bicarbonate of soda, salt and sugar into a large bowl. Mix the milk and cream of tartar in a jug. Add the melted butter and egg to the flour with the walnuts and dates. Gradually mix in the milk to make a soft dough.

2 Tip out on to a lightly floured surface, knead briefly then pat into a 20 cm circle. Transfer to a greased baking sheet and make a cross cut on top of the dough.

3 Sprinkle with a little extra flour and bake immediately in a preheated oven, 220°C (425°F), Gas Mark 7, for 25–30 minutes until the bread is browned and sounds hollow when tapped with the fingertips.

4 Transfer to a wire rack to cool.

prep + cook time 35–40 minutes
makes 1 large loaf
tip For a soft crust, wrap the hot bread in a clean tea towel and leave to cool.

GLUTEN-FREE SPICY FRUIT & SEED BREAD

150g chickpea flour
150g gluten-free flour
2 teaspoons fast-action dried
   yeast
1 teaspoon salt
1 teaspoon caster sugar
1 tablespoon black onion seeds
1 tablespoon cumin seeds
2 teaspoons ground coriander
¼ teaspoon dried chilli flakes
50g dried mango or pear,
   chopped
2 tablespoons groundnut oil
200ml warm water

1 Place the flours, yeast, salt, sugar, spices and dried fruit in a bowl and stir to combine. Mix together the oil and water in a separate bowl, add to the dry ingredients and combine to form a stiff dough.

2 Spoon the mixture into a greased 500g (1lb) tin, cover loosely with oiled cling film and leave in a warm place to rise for about 45 minutes or until the mixture is slightly above the top of the tin.

3 Place in a preheated oven, 200°C (400°F), Gas Mark 6, for 20–25 minutes until firm to the touch. Transfer to a wire rack to cool.

prep + cook time 30–35 minutes + proving time
makes 1 small loaf

GINGERED FIG & ORANGE BREAD

1 large orange, freshly squeezed
    or 200ml fresh, shop-bought
    orange juice
150g dried figs, chopped
175g strong wholemeal bread
    flour
300g strong white bread flour
2 tablespoons butter
1 teaspoon salt
1¼ teaspoons fast-action dried
    yeast
4 tablespoons thick set honey
150ml warm water
4 teaspoons chopped crystallised
    ginger
milk, to glaze

1 Warm the orange juice in a
small saucepan, add the chopped
figs and set aside for 30 minutes.
2 Put the flours into a large bowl,
add the butter and rub in with
the fingertips until the mixture
resembles fine breadcrumbs. Stir
in the salt and yeast then add the
honey. Drain the orange juice and
add to the bowl then gradually
mix in enough warm water to
make a soft dough.
3 Knead well on a lightly floured
surface for 5 minutes until the
dough is smooth and elastic.
Gradually work in the soaked figs
and the ginger. Put the dough
back into the bowl, cover loosely
with oiled cling film and leave in
a warm place to rise for 1 hour or
until doubled in size.
4 Tip the dough out on to a
lightly floured surface, knead well
then shape into an oval and press
into a greased 1.8 litre loaf tin.
Cover loosely with oiled cling
film and leave in a warm place
to rise for 30 minutes or until the
dough reaches just above the top
of the tin.

5 Remove the cling film, brush
with milk and bake in a preheated
oven, 200°C (400°F), Gas Mark 6,
for 35–40 minutes until the bread
is well risen, deep brown in colour
and sounds hollow when tapped
with the fingertips. Cover with
foil after 15 minutes to prevent
overbrowning.
6 Transfer to a wire rack to cool.

prep + cook time 45–50 minutes
+ standing, kneading and proving
time
makes 1 extra large loaf

CHOCOLATE & PECAN SPIRAL

500g strong white bread flour
3 tablespoons butter
½ teaspoon salt
50g caster sugar
1½ teaspoon fast-action dried
    yeast
2 eggs, beaten
175ml warm milk

filling
125g plain dark chocolate, finely
    chopped
125g pecan nuts, roughly
    chopped
2 tablespoons caster sugar
1 egg yolk, to glaze

1 Put the flour into a large bowl, add the butter and rub in with the fingertips until the mixture resembles fine breadcrumbs. Stir in the salt, sugar and yeast. Add the beaten eggs and gradually mix in enough warm milk to make a soft dough.

2 Knead well on a lightly floured surface for 5 minutes until the dough is smooth and elastic. Put the dough back into the bowl, cover loosely with oiled cling film and leave in a warm place to rise for 1 hour or until doubled in size.

3 Tip the dough out on to a lightly floured surface, knead well then roll out to a 27cm square. Sprinkle with three quarters of the chocolate and nuts, and all the sugar.

4 Roll up the dough then put it into a greased 1.8 litre loaf tin. Cover loosely with oiled cling film and leave in a warm place for 30 minutes or until the dough reaches just above the top of the tin.

5 Remove the cling film, brush with the egg yolk mixed with 1 tablespoon of water and sprinkle with the remaining chocolate and pecan nuts. Bake in a preheated oven, 200°C (400°F), Gas Mark 6, for 35–40 minutes until the bread is well risen and deep brown and sounds hollow when tapped with the fingertips. Cover with foil after 10 minutes to prevent the nuts overbrowning.

6 Transfer to a wire rack to cool.

prep + cook time 45–50 minutes + kneading and proving time
makes 1 extra large loaf

THREE KINGS RING

500g strong white bread flour

1 teaspoon salt

1 orange, grated rind only

1 lemon, grated rind only

125g caster sugar

1½ teaspoons fast-action dried
  yeast

75g butter, melted

2 eggs, beaten

175ml warm milk

100g whole candied peel

125g glacé cherries

125g blanched almonds, cut into
  slivers

1 egg yolk, to glaze

to finish

125g icing sugar

4–5 teaspoons orange or lemon
  juice

1 Put the flour in a large bowl then stir in the salt, grated fruit rinds, sugar and yeast. Add the melted butter and beaten eggs then gradually mix in enough warm water to make a soft dough.
2 Knead well on a lightly floured surface until the dough is smooth and elastic. Put back into the bowl and cover with oiled cling film. Leave in a warm place to rise for 1¼ hours or until doubled in size.
3 Tip the dough out on to a lightly floured surface and knead well. Roughly chop the candied peel, cherries and almonds. Reserve one-third of the mixture then gradually knead the remainder into the dough.
4 Shape the dough into a thick rope 50 cm long and squeeze together the ends to make a ring. Place on to a greased baking sheet. Stand a greased, heatproof bowl in the centre of the ring to keep the hole shape and cover loosely with oiled cling film. Leave to rise for 30 minutes or until half as big again.
5 Remove the cling film and bowl. Brush with the egg yolk mixed

with 1 tablespoon of water. Bake in a preheated oven, 200°C (400°F), Gas Mark 6, for 20–25 minutes until the bread is golden brown and sounds hollow when tapped with the fingertips. Cover with foil if overbrowning.
6 Transfer to a wire rack to cool. Sift the icing sugar into a bowl then gradually mix in the orange or lemon juice to make a smooth, pouring icing. Drizzle over the bread in random lines. Sprinkle with the reserved fruit and nuts then leave to set.

prep + cook time 45–50 minutes + kneading, proving and shaping time
makes 1 large loaf
tips This rich, sweet bread is made in Spanish-speaking countries to mark Epiphany. Traditionally, it contains a dried pea and two other tiny foil-wrapped gifts. If you do add any gifts, make sure they are heatproof. Wrap them in foil and press into the underside of the dough before proving the loaf. Remember to warn your guests to watch out for the gifts.

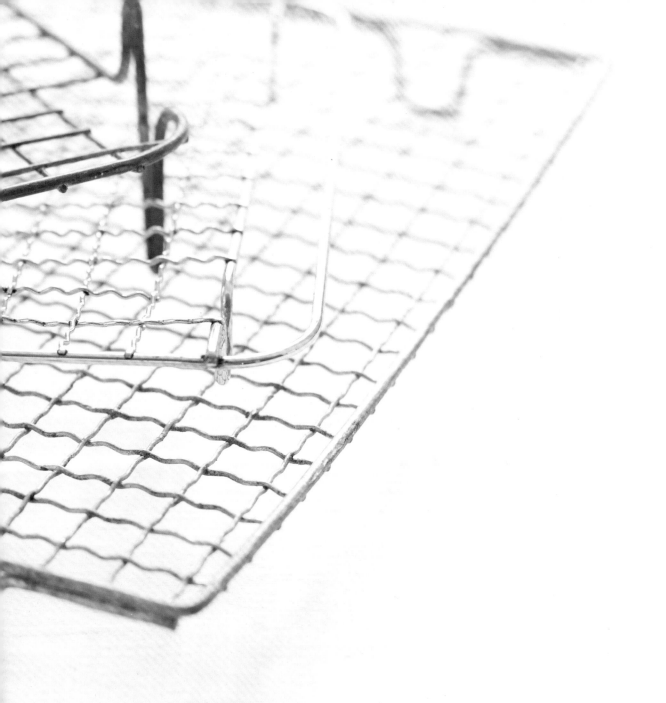

LITTLE BREADS

WHOLEMEAL ROLLS

500g strong wholemeal bread
   flour
250g strong white bread flour,
   sifted
7g sachet fast-action dried yeast
2 teaspoons salt
1 teaspoon caster sugar
450ml warm water
2 tablespoons milk

1 Put the flours, yeast, salt and sugar into a large bowl. Add the warm water and bring the ingredients together until they form a soft dough. Knead for 8–10 minutes until it is smooth and elastic.

2 Shape into a ball and put the dough back into the bowl, cover loosely with oiled cling film and leave in a warm place to rise for 1 hour or until doubled in size.

3 Turn out the dough on to a lightly floured surface and knock out the air. Divide the dough into 8 equal pieces and shape these into rolls. Arrange them well spaced apart on 2 large, lightly greased baking sheets, cover with oiled cling film and leave to rise for 30 minutes until they have doubled in size.

4 Brush the rolls with the milk and bake in a preheated oven, 220°C (425°F), Gas Mark 7, for 20 minutes until they are risen and sound hollow when tapped underneath. Transfer to a wire rack to cool.

prep + cook time 30 minutes + kneading, proving and shaping time

makes 8 large rolls

tip You can make this recipe into a wholemeal loaf by shaping the dough into your preferred shape and baking it for 25–30 minutes until it sounds hollow when tapped.

FANCY ROLLS

475g strong white bread flour
2 tablespoons butter
1 teaspoon granulated sugar
1 teaspoon salt
1¼ teaspoons fast-action dried
   yeast
275ml warm water

to finish
1 egg yolk, to glaze
poppy or black mustard seeds,
   sesame seeds, fennel seeds,
   paprika, sprigs of fresh
   rosemary, coarsely ground
   Cajun spice, coarse sea salt

1 Put the flour into a bowl, add the butter and rub in with the fingertips until the mixture resembles fine breadcrumbs. Stir in the sugar, salt and yeast then gradually mix in enough warm water to make a soft dough.
2 Knead well on a lightly floured surface for 5 minutes until the dough is smooth and elastic. Put the dough back into the bowl, cover loosely with oiled cling film and leave in a warm place to rise for 1 hour or until doubled in size.
3 Tip the dough out on to a lightly floured surface, knead well then cut into 12 pieces. Shape them as below then put on to greased baking sheets.
4 Cover loosely with oiled cling film and leave in a warm place to rise for 20 minutes.
5 Remove the cling film, brush with the egg yolk mixed with 1 tablespoon of water and sprinkle with seeds, spices, herbs or salt. Bake in a preheated oven, 200°C (400°F), Gas Mark 6, for 10 minutes until golden and the bases sound hollow when tapped with the fingertips. Transfer to a wire rack to cool.

prep + cook time 25 minutes + kneading, proving and shaping time
makes 12 rolls

coils Take 2 pieces of dough and shape each one into a rope 25cm long, roll up each rope along its length to make a spiral-like coil.
clover leaf Take 2 pieces of dough and divide each one into 3 small balls, arrange in a triangle with the balls all touching each other.
starburst Take 2 pieces of dough and shape each into a round. Make 5 or 6 cuts with scissors towards the centre of each one to resemble the spokes of a wheel.
knots Take 2 pieces of dough and shape each one into a rope 22 cm long. Loop one end of one rope then thread the other end through the loop to make the knot. Repeat.
herb split Take 2 pieces of dough and shape into an oval. Make 4 small cuts across the top of each with scissors and insert sprigs of rosemary into them. (Add fresh sprigs after baking too.)

MINI BARLEY FLOWER POT LOAVES

400g strong coarse brown bread
flour
2 tablespoons butter
1 teaspoon salt
1 teaspoon caster sugar
2 tablespoons milk powder
50g barley flakes
1¼ teaspoons fast-action dried
yeast
2 tablespoons barley malt extract
275ml warm water
2 tablespoons milk, to glaze
extra barley flakes, to sprinkle

1 Put the flour into a large bowl, add the butter and rub in with the fingertips until the mixture resembles fine breadcrumbs. Stir in the salt, sugar, milk powder, barley flakes and yeast. Add the malt extract and enough warm water to make a soft dough.
2 Knead well on a lightly floured surface for 5 minutes until the dough is smooth and elastic. Put it back into the bowl, cover loosely with oiled cling film and leave in a warm place for 1 hour or until doubled in size.
3 Tip the dough out on to a lightly floured surface and knead well. Cut into 10 pieces and shape each into a ball. Press into 10 greased 150ml individual plain dessert moulds or large dariole tins.
4 Transfer the moulds to a baking sheet. Cover loosely with oiled cling film and leave in a warm place to rise for 30 minutes or until the dough reaches just above the top of the tins.

5 Remove the cling film, brush the tops with milk and sprinkle with a few extra barley flakes. Bake in a preheated oven, 200°C (400°F), Gas Mark 6, for 12–15 minutes until the breads are well risen, browned and sound hollow when tapped with the fingertips.
6 Transfer to a wire rack to cool.

prep + cook time about 25 minutes + kneading, proving and shaping time
makes 10 mini loaves
tip Barley malt extract is available from health food shops and some supermarkets.

DRIZZLED ORANGE & POPPY SEED BUNS

500g strong white bread flour
2 tablespoons butter
2 tablespoons milk powder
1 teaspoon salt
40g poppy seeds
1 orange, grated rind and juice
1¼ teaspoons fast-action dried
  yeast
4 tablespoons honey
275ml warm water
1 egg yolk, to glaze
200g icing sugar

1 Put the flour into a large bowl, add the butter and rub in with the fingertips until the mixture resembles fine breadcrumbs. Stir in the milk powder, salt, poppy seeds, grated orange rind and yeast. Add the honey then gradually mix in enough warm water to make a soft, sticky dough.
2 Knead well on a lightly floured surface for 5 minutes until the dough is smooth and elastic. Put the dough back into the bowl, cover loosely with oiled cling film and leave in a warm place to rise for 1 hour or until doubled in size.
3 Tip the dough out on to a lightly floured surface, knead well then cut into 20 pieces. Shape each piece into a small ball and arrange, spaced well apart, on a greased baking sheet.
4 Cover loosely with oiled cling film and leave to rise for 30 minutes or until half as big again.
5 Remove the cling film, brush with the egg yolk mixed with 1 tablespoon of water and bake in a preheated oven, 200°C (400°F), Gas Mark 6, for 12–15 minutes until the buns are golden and sound hollow when tapped with the fingertips. Transfer to a wire rack and leave to cool for 15 minutes.
6 Sift the icing sugar into a bowl then gradually mix in the juice of half the orange or enough to make a smooth spoonable icing. Drizzle the icing over the buns with a spoon making random zigzag lines. Leave for at least 15 minutes so that the icing can harden.

prep + cook time about 25 minutes + kneading, proving and shaping time
makes 20 buns
tip Instead of the poppy seeds, try adding 125g roughly chopped glacé cherries when kneading the dough for the first time.

YOGURT, CHEDDAR & ROSEMARY MUFFINS

250g strong wholemeal bread
    flour
125g strong white bread flour
125g buckwheat flour
2 teaspoons salt
1½ teaspoons baking powder
½ teaspoon bicarbonate of soda,
2 tablespoons chopped fresh
    rosemary
50g melted butter
2 eggs, beaten
100ml natural yogurt
100ml milk
75g Cheddar cheese, grated
8 small sprigs fresh rosemary

1 Put all the dry ingredients in a large bowl and mix well. Make a well in the centre. Beat together the remaining ingredients (except the rosemary sprigs) and pour them into the dry ingredients. Mix together until they form a sticky dough.

2 Lightly grease an 8-hole mini-loaf tin. Take large spoonfuls of the mixture and press into the prepared tins. Press a rosemary sprig into each one.

3 Bake in a preheated oven, 190°C (375°F), Gas Mark 5, for 20–25 minutes until risen and lightly golden. Leave to cool in the tins for 5 minutes, then transfer to a wire rack to cool.

prep + cook time 40–45 minutes
makes 12 muffins

CHOCOLATE BRIOCHE BUNS

500g strong white bread flour
1 teaspoon salt
7g sachet fast-action dried yeast
50g caster sugar
125g unsalted butter, melted
5 eggs, lightly beaten
12 squares dark chocolate

egg glaze
1 egg beaten into 2 tablespoons
   milk

1 Sift the flour and salt into a large bowl and stir in the yeast and sugar. Add the melted butter and eggs. Mix together to form a soft, sticky dough.

2 Knead well on a lightly floured surface for 8–10 minutes until smooth and elastic. Shape the dough into a ball and put back into the bowl, cover loosely with oiled cling film and leave in a warm place to rise for 1 hour or until doubled in size.

3 Turn out the dough on to a lightly floured surface. Cut off and reserve 250g of the dough and divide the rest into 12 equal pieces. Shape each piece into a bun and then flatten it out, placing a piece of chocolate in the centre. Fold the edges over the chocolate, pinching them together to seal. Press the buns, seam side down, into 12 lightly greased individual brioche tins.

4 Take the reserved dough and divide it into 12 small pieces. Shape each into a ball. Make a small indentation in the top of each bun, brush with a little of the egg glaze and press a small ball of dough into each one. Cover the tins with oiled cling film and leave to rise for 30 minutes until the buns have doubled in size.

5 Bake in a preheated oven, 190°C (375°F), Gas Mark 5, for 20 minutes until the buns are risen and sound hollow when tapped underneath. Remove them from the tins and transfer to a wire rack to cool.

prep + cook time about 30 minutes + kneading, proving and shaping time
makes 12 buns
tip Traditional brioches are made in fluted moulds as individual loaves or as small buns. If you don't have small brioche moulds they can be made in a muffin tray.

BABY PANETTONES

2 teaspoons easy-blend dried
   yeast
125g caster sugar, plus
   1 teaspoon
175ml warm milk
700g strong white bread flour
4 large eggs, plus 2 yolks
2 teaspoons vanilla extract
finely grated rind of 2 lemons
175g salted butter, very soft and
   diced
175g mixed dried fruit

1 Grease 8 x 400ml clean food cans and line with baking parchment that extends above the rims. Grease the paper. Stir the yeast and 1 teaspoon sugar into the milk in a large, warm bowl and leave for 10 minutes or until frothy. Stir in 100g of the flour. Cover with oiled cling film and leave for 30 minutes.

2 Add the eggs and yolks, the remaining flour and the sugar, vanilla extract, lemon rind and butter. Mix with a round-bladed knife to make a soft dough, adding a little more flour if the dough feels sticky. Turn out on to a lightly floured surface and knead until smooth and elastic. Put the dough back into the bowl, cover loosely with oiled cling film and leave in a warm place to rise for 2–4 hours or until doubled in size.

3 Knock back the dough and lightly knead in the dried fruit. Cut the dough into 8 pieces and drop into the tins. Cover with oiled cling film and leave to rise until the dough almost reaches the rims.

4 Bake in a preheated oven, 200°C (400°F), Gas Mark 6, for 20–25 minutes or until risen and golden. Leave for 5 minutes, then cool on a wire rack.

makes 8 panettone
Preparation time 25 minutes, plus rising
Cooking time 20–25 minutes
tip For whole panettone, shape the mixture into 1 large ball. Place in a 15cm round cake tin, greased and lined with a double layer of greased baking parchment that extends 10cm above the rim. Cover and leave to rise. Bake for 15 minutes at 200°C (400°F), Gas Mark 6, then reduce to 180°C (350°F), Gas Mark 4, and bake for 40 minutes until well risen and an inserted skewer comes out clean. Leave for 10 minutes, then cool on a wire rack.

HOT CROSS BUNS

750g strong white bread flour, sifted
2 x 7g sachets fast-action dried yeast
2 teaspoons ground mixed spice
1 teaspoon ground cinnamon
100g raisins
75g cut mixed peel
100g caster sugar
350ml warm milk
50g unsalted butter, melted
1 egg, lightly beaten

apricot glaze
125g apricot jam
1 teaspoon lemon juice
1 teaspoon water

piping paste
50g plain flour
1 tablespoon caster sugar
3 tablespoons water

1 Sift the flour into a large bowl and stir in the yeast, spices, raisins, peel and sugar. Add the milk, melted butter and egg. Mix together to form a soft, sticky dough.

2 Knead well on a lightly floured surface for 8–10 minutes until smooth and elastic. Shape the dough into a ball and put back into the bowl, cover loosely with oiled cling film and leave in a warm place to rise for 1 hour or until doubled in size.

3 Knock back the dough on a lightly floured surface. Divide into 12 equal-sized pieces and shape each one into a small bun. Press the buns into a lightly greased 20 x 30cm cake tin. Cover with oiled cling film and leave to rise for a further 30 minutes until the dough doubles in size.

4 Make the piping paste. Mix the flour, sugar and water to form a paste and spoon into a paper icing bag. Pipe the paste over the buns to form crosses.

5 Make the apricot glaze. Put the jam in a small saucepan with the lemon juice and water and heat gently until the jam melts.

Increase the heat and boil for 1 minute, remove from the heat and press through a fine sieve. Keep warm until needed.

6 Bake the buns in a preheated oven, 200°C (400°F), Gas Mark 6, for 30–35 minutes until risen and golden, covering the tin loosely with foil if the buns start to brown. Remove from the oven, brush each bun with apricot glaze and transfer to a wire rack to cool.

prep + cook time about 45 minutes + kneading, proving and shaping time
makes 12 buns

BREAD MAKER
BAKING

SPEEDY SESAME BREAD

275ml warm water
2 tablespoons sunflower oil
1 teaspoon salt
2 tablespoons milk powder
2 tablespoons sesame seeds
475g strong white bread flour
1 tablespoon caster sugar
2½ teaspoons fast-action dried
   yeast

to finish
melted butter, to brush
sesame seeds, for sprinkling

1 Lift the bread pan out of the machine and fit the blade. Put the dough ingredients in the pan, following the order specified in the manual.

2 Fit the pan into the machine and close the lid. Set to a 750g (1½lb) loaf size on the fast/rapid bake programme.

3 At the end of the programme lift the pan out of the machine and shake the bread out on to a wire rack. Brush the top of the loaf with the butter and sprinkle with a few extra sesame seeds. Brown under the grill, if liked.

prep + cook time 1–2 hours, depending on machine
makes 1 large loaf

OATMEAL & BUTTERMILK BREAD

125ml water
175ml buttermilk
1½ teaspoons salt
425g strong white bread flour
50g fine or medium oatmeal,
    plus extra for sprinkling
1½ teaspoons caster sugar
1¼ teaspoons fast-action
    dried yeast
milk, to brush

1 Lift the bread pan out of the machine and fit the blade. Put the ingredients in the pan, following the order specified in the manual.
2 Fit the pan into the machine and close the lid. Set to a 750g (1½lb) loaf size on the basic white programme. Select your preferred crust setting.
3 Just before baking begins brush the top of the dough lightly with milk and sprinkle with extra oatmeal. Close the lid gently.
4 At the end of the programme lift the pan out of the machine and shake the bread out on to a wire rack to cool.

prep + cook time 3–4 hours, depending on machine
makes 1 large loaf

FAST-BAKED RYE & CARAWAY BREAD

200ml warm water
200ml natural Greek yogurt
1½ teaspoons salt
1 tablespoon caraway seeds
325g strong white bread flour
175g rye flour
1 tablespoon caster sugar
2½ teaspoons fast-action dried
  yeast

1 Lift the bread pan out of the machine and fit the blade. Put the ingredients in the pan, following the order specified in the manual.
2 Fit the pan into the machine and close the lid. Set to a 750g (1½lb) loaf size on the fast/rapid bake programme.
3 At the end of the programme lift the pan out of the machine and shake the bread out on to a wire rack to cool. Serve thinly sliced.

prep + cook time 1–2 hours, depending on machine
makes 1 large loaf

DATE & MALTED BARLEY BREAD

250ml milk, plus 1 tablespoon
  to brush
5 tablespoons date syrup or
  barley malt extract
25g unsalted butter, softened
1 teaspoon salt
325g barley flour
150g strong white bread flour
1¼ teaspoons fast-action dried
  yeast
150g pitted dates, chopped
barley flakes, for sprinkling
  (optional)

1 Lift the bread pan out of the machine and fit the blade. Put the ingredients, except the dates, in the pan, following the order specified in the manual.

2 Fit the pan into the machine and set to a 750g (1½lb) loaf size on the sweet programme (or the wholemeal programme if the machine doesn't have a sweet setting). Add the dates when the machine beeps.

3 Just before baking begins brush the top of the dough lightly with milk and sprinkle with barley flakes (if liked). Close the lid gently.

4 At the end of the programme lift the pan out of the machine and shake the bread out on to a wire rack to cool.

prep + cook time 2¾–3½ hours, depending on machine
makes 1 large loaf
tip Barley malt extract and date syrup are available from health food shops and some supermarkets.

CHILLI & SMOKED PAPRIKA BREAD

275ml water
2 tablespoons olive oil
1 teaspoon salt
1 teaspoon smoked paprika
1 large mild fresh red chilli,
    halved, deseeded and finely
    chopped
300g strong white bread flour
150g strong wholemeal bread
    flour
1 teaspoon caster sugar
1¼ teaspoons fast-action dried
    yeast
50g sun-dried tomatoes in oil,
    drained and roughly chopped
    (optional)

1 Lift the bread pan out of the machine and fit the blade. Put the ingredients, except the sun-dried tomatoes, in the pan following the order specified in the manual.
2 Fit the pan into the machine and close the lid. Set to a 750g (1½lb) loaf size on the basic white programme. Select your preferred crust setting. Add the sun-dried tomatoes (if using) when the machine beeps.
3 At the end of the programme lift the pan out of the machine and shake the bread out on to a wire rack to cool.

prep + cook time 3–4 hours, depending on machine
makes 1 large loaf

ONION & TOMATO SCHIACCIATA

dough
275ml water
3 tablespoons olive oil
1 teaspoon salt
475g strong white bread flour
2 teaspoons caster sugar
1½ teaspoons fast-action dried
  yeast

to finish
4 tablespoons olive oil
1 large red onion, thinly sliced
2 garlic cloves, finely chopped
1 teaspoon caster sugar
3 teaspoons black olive pesto or
  sun-dried tomato pesto
50g sun-dried tomatoes in oil,
  drained and sliced
small bunch of basil
coarse salt flakes

1 Lift the bread pan out of the machine and fit the blade. Put the dough ingredients in the pan, following the order specified in the manual. Fit the pan into the machine and close the lid. Set to the dough programme.
2 Heat 1 tablespoon oil in a frying pan. Add the onion and garlic and fry gently for 5 minutes until softened. Scoop out one-quarter and reserve for the topping. Add the sugar to the remaining onions and cook for a few minutes more until caramelised.
3 At the end of the programme turn the dough out on to a floured surface and cut it in half. Roll one half to a 23cm round. Place on an greased baking sheet. Spread with the pesto. Top with the caramelised onions, three-quarters of the sun-dried tomatoes, half the basil leaves and drizzle with 2 tablespoons oil.
4 Roll out the remaining dough to a circle and cover the first circle. Sprinkle with the remaining onions, tomatoes, basil leaves and a little salt. Cover loosely with oiled cling film and leave to rise in a warm place for 30 minutes.

5 Bake in a preheated oven, 200°C (400°F), Gas Mark 6, for 25 minutes until golden brown and the centre is cooked through. Transfer to a chopping board, drizzle with the remaining oil and serve warm, cut into wedges.

prep + cook time about 1½–2½ hours, depending on machine + shaping and proving time
makes 1 round loaf

MINTED COURGETTE & LEMON LOAF

1 large courgette, about 225g

2 tablespoons salt, plus
 ½ teaspoon

175ml water

75ml olive oil

½ teaspoon black pepper

grated rind of 1 lemon

2 tablespoons chopped mint

3 tablespoons capers, rinsed and
 drained

400g strong white bread flour

1 tablespoon caster sugar

1¼ teaspoons fast-action dried
 yeast

1 Coarsely grate the courgette and mix in a colander with 2 tablespoons salt. Leave to stand for 30 minutes. Rinse the courgette in plenty of cold water and pat dry between several layers of kitchen paper.

2 Lift the bread pan out of the machine and fit the blade. Put the ingredients in the pan, following the order specified in the manual.

3 Fit the pan into the machine and close the lid. Set to a 750g (1½lb) loaf size on the basic white programme. Select your preferred crust setting. Add the courgette, lemon, mint and capers when the machine beeps.

4 At the end of the programme lift the pan out of the machine and shake the bread out on to a wire rack to cool.

prep + cook time 3–4 hours, depending on machine + standing time
makes 1 large loaf

CHILLI CHOCOLATE BREAD

250ml water
3 tablespoons sunflower oil
1½ teaspoons salt
1½ teaspoons crushed dried
    chillies
½ teaspoon ground cinnamon
75g plain dark chocolate
    (85% cocoa solids), grated
1 tablespoon cocoa powder
350g strong white bread flour
50g cornmeal
2 tablespoons molasses sugar
1 teaspoon fast-action dried yeast

1 Lift the bread pan out of the machine and fit the blade. Put the ingredients in the pan, following the order specified in the manual. Add the spices, grated chocolate and cocoa powder with the flour.
2 Fit the pan into the machine and close the lid. Set to a 750g (1½lb) loaf size on the basic white programme. Select your preferred crust setting.
3 At the end of the programme lift the pan out of the machine and shake the bread out on to a wire rack to cool.

prep + cook time 3–4 hours, depending on machine
makes 1 large loaf

SPINACH & MANCHEGO RING LOAF

dough

2 tablespoons olive oil

1 small onion, finely chopped

250ml water

25g Parmesan cheese, grated, plus extra for sprinkling

1 teaspoon salt

450g strong white bread flour

1 tablespoon caster sugar

1½ teaspoons fast-action dried yeast

to finish

175g young spinach leaves

200g Manchego cheese, cut into small dice

½ teaspoon freshly grated nutmeg

2 garlic cloves, finely chopped

50g raisins

50g pine nuts, lightly toasted

beaten egg, to glaze

salt and black pepper

1 Heat the oil in a frying pan and gently fry the onion until softened. Leave to cool.

2 Lift the bread pan out of the machine and fit the blade. Put the dough ingredients in the pan, following the order specified in the manual. Add the onion and cheese with the water. Fit the pan into the machine and close the lid. Set to the dough programme.

3 Put the spinach in a saucepan with 1 tablespoon water and cover with a lid. Heat gently until the spinach has wilted. Drain and pat the spinach dry between layers of kitchen paper. In a bowl, mix together the Manchego with the nutmeg, garlic, raisins, pine nuts and seasoning.

4 At the end of the programme turn the dough out on to a lightly floured surface and roll it out to a rectangle, about 40 x 30cm. Spread the filling almost to the edges. Roll up the dough, starting from a long side. Transfer the roll to a large, greased baking sheet with the join underneath. Bend the ends round to make a ring and push the ends firmly together to

seal. Cover loosely with oiled cling film and leave in a warm place for about 45 minutes until risen by at least half again.

5 Brush the dough with beaten egg to glaze and sprinkle with extra grated Parmesan. Make vertical scores to the middle of the dough so that the filling is revealed. Bake in a preheated oven, 200°C (400°F), Gas Mark 6, for 30–35 minutes until risen and golden. Serve warm or cold.

prep + cook time 1½–2½ hours, depending on machine + shaping and proving time

makes 1 large ring loaf (about 10 thick slices)

SEEDED NAAN BREADS

12 cardamom pods
2 teaspoons coriander seeds
2 teaspoons cumin seeds
100ml water
4 tablespoons natural yogurt
1 tablespoon vegetable oil
1 teaspoon salt
2 teaspoons black onion seeds
275g strong white bread flour
1 teaspoon caster sugar
¾ teaspoon fast-action dried
   yeast
flour, for dusting
25g butter or ghee, melted

1 Crush the cardamom pods using a pestle and mortar to release the seeds. Discard the shells. Add the coriander and cumin seeds and grind until crushed.
2 Lift the bread pan out of the machine and fit the blade. Put the ingredients, except the butter or ghee, in the pan, following the order specified in the manual. Add all the seeds with the flour. Fit the pan into the machine and close the lid. Set to the dough programme.
3 At the end of the programme turn the dough out on to a lightly floured surface and divide it into 6 pieces. Roll each out to a tear shape about 22cm long. Place on floured trays; dust with flour. Cover loosely with a clean, dry teatowel and leave to rise in a warm place for 20 minutes.

4 Preheat the grill to its highest setting and heat a large baking sheet under the grill. Brush the dough with the butter or ghee and cook on the baking sheet in 2 or 3 batches until puffy and patchily brown. Stack the cooked breads on a plate and cover with a clean, dry tea towel while you cook the remainder.

prep + cook time 1½–2½ hours, depending on machine + shaping and proving time
makes 6 naan breads

ASIAN-STYLE FLATBREADS

50g sesame seeds
225ml water
1 garlic clove, chopped
25g fresh root ginger, grated
25g roughly chopped fresh
  coriander
2 tablespoons sesame oil
2 teaspoons salt
450g strong white bread flour
1 tablespoon caster sugar
1¼ teaspoons fast-action dried
  yeast

1 Put the sesame seeds in a food processor and grind until broken up. (The seeds won't grind to a powder.)
2 Lift the bread pan out of the machine and fit the blade. Put the ingredients in the pan, following the order specified in the manual. Add the seeds, garlic, ginger and coriander with the water.
3 Fit the pan into the machine and close the lid. Set to the dough programme.
4 At the end of the programme turn the dough out on to a lightly floured surface and divide it into 8 equal pieces. Roll out each piece to a circle 20cm across. Leave the rounds on the floured surface, covered with a clean, dry tea towel, for 15 minutes.
5 Heat a large frying pan or griddle, then reduce to the lowest setting. Place a piece of dough in the pan and cook for 3–4 minutes, turning once, until golden brown in places. Slide the bread on to a plate and cover with a clean, damp tea towel while you cook the rest.

prep + cook time 1½–2½ hours, depending on machine + shaping and proving time
makes 8 breads

SALTED PRETZELS

dough
275ml milk
1 teaspoon salt
300g strong white bread flour
75g rye flour
1 tablespoon caster sugar
1 teaspoon fast-action dried yeast

to finish
4 teaspoons sea salt
2 teaspoons caster sugar

1 Lift the bread pan out of the machine and fit the blade. Put the dough ingredients in the pan, following the order specified in the manual. Fit the pan into the machine and close the lid. Set to the dough programme.

2 Put 2 teaspoons sea salt in a small saucepan with the sugar and 3 tablespoons water. Heat until the salt and sugar dissolve, then turn into a small bowl. Grease 2 baking sheets.

3 At the end of the programme turn the dough out on to a lightly floured surface and roll it out to a rectangle, about 35 x 25cm. Cover loosely with a clean, dry tea towel and leave to stand for 20 minutes. Cut the rectangle across at 1cm intervals. Take a piece of dough and bend the ends around to meet, twisting the ends together. Press the ends down on to the curved side of the rope to shape the pretzel. Use the remaining dough to make more pretzels and place them on 2 large, greased baking sheets. Cover loosely with oiled cling film and leave for a further 20 minutes.

4 Bake in a preheated oven, 220°C (425°F), Gas Mark 7, for 8 minutes until golden. Brush with the salt glaze and sprinkle with more salt. Cool on a wire rack.

prep + cook time 1½–2½ hours, depending on machine + shaping and proving time
makes 35–40 pretzels

SALT & PEPPER CRUSTED ROLLS

275ml water
25g unsalted butter, softened
475g strong white bread flour
1 teaspoon caster sugar
1¼ teaspoons fast-action dried
  yeast
2 teaspoons sea salt
2 teaspoons multi-coloured
  peppercorns, crushed
1 tablespoon semolina flour
milk, to brush

1 Lift the bread pan out of the machine and fit the blade. Add the water, butter, flour, sugar, yeast and ½ teaspoon of the salt to the pan, following the order specified in the manual.
2 Fit the pan into the machine and close the lid. Set to the dough programme.
3 Mix the remaining salt with the pepper and semolina and sprinkle on a plate.
4 At the end of the programme turn the dough out on to a lightly floured surface and cut it into 12 equal pieces. Shape each into a ball and brush the tops lightly with milk. Dip in the salt and pepper mixture and then space them about 4cm apart on a large, greased baking sheet. Cover loosely with a clean, dry tea towel and leave to rise in a warm place for 30 minutes.
5 Bake in a preheated oven, 220°C (425°F), Gas Mark 7, for about 10 minutes until risen and golden. Transfer to a wire rack to cool.

prep + cook time 1½–2½ hours, depending on machine + shaping and proving time
makes 12 rolls

GOATS' CHEESE & BEAN MINI LOAVES

dough

275ml water

3 tablespoons olive oil

3 tablespoons snipped chives

½ teaspoon black pepper, plus
  extra for sprinkling

1½ teaspoons salt

475g strong white bread flour

1 teaspoon caster sugar

1¼ teaspoons fast-action dried
  yeast

to finish

100g frozen baby broad beans
  or soya beans

200g soft goats' cheese, diced

milk, to brush

1 Lift the bread pan out of the machine and fit the blade. Put the dough ingredients in the pan, following the order specified in the manual.

2 Fit the pan into the machine and close the lid. Set to the dough programme.

3 Cook the beans in boiling water for 1 minute. Rinse in cold water and pat dry on kitchen paper.

4 At the end of the programme turn the dough out on to a lightly floured surface, scatter with the beans and cheese and knead them into the dough until evenly distributed. Cut the dough into 10 equal pieces.

5 Grease 10 individual loaf tins and place them on a baking sheet. Press each piece of dough into a tin. (If you don't have any individual tins, shape the dough into balls and space them slightly apart on the baking sheet.) Cover loosely with oiled cling film and leave to rise in a warm place for 30–40 minutes or until almost doubled in size.

6 Brush with a little milk, sprinkle with extra black pepper and bake in a preheated oven, 220°C (425°F), Gas Mark 7, for 20–25 minutes until risen and pale golden. Transfer to a wire rack to cool.

prep + cook time 1½–2½ hours, depending on machine + shaping and proving time
makes 10 mini loaves

DEVONSHIRE SPLITS

dough

300ml cold water

2 tablespoons butter, at room
    temperature

½ teaspoon salt

2 tablespoons milk powder

500g strong white bread flour

2 teaspoons caster sugar

1¼ teaspoons fast-action dried
    yeast

to finish

beaten egg, to glaze

250g strawberry jam

250g clotted cream

icing sugar, for dusting

1 Lift the bread pan out of the machine and fit the blade. Put the dough ingredients in the pan, following the order specified in the manual.

2 Fit the pan into the machine and close the lid. Set to the dough programme.

3 At the end of the programme turn the dough out on to a lightly floured surface and cut it into 12 pieces. Shape each piece into a ball. Put them on large, greased baking sheets, leaving a little space around each one. Cover loosely with oiled cling film and leave to rise in a warm place for 20–30 minutes.

4 Brush the rolls with beaten egg. Bake in a preheated oven, 200°C (400°F), Gas Mark 6, for 10 minutes until golden and the bases sound hollow when tapped with the fingertips. Transfer to a wire rack to cool.

5 When ready to serve, cut a diagonal slice down through the rolls almost but not quite through to the base. Spoon the jam into the slit, then add spoonfuls of clotted cream. Transfer to serving plates and dust with icing sugar.

prep + cook time 1½–2½ hours, depending on machine + shaping and proving time
makes 12 splits

WHITE CHOCOLATE & BANANA LOAF

225g mashed banana (about
  2 large bananas)
150ml warm milk
50g unsalted butter, softened
½ teaspoon salt
425g strong white bread flour
50g caster sugar
2½ teaspoons fast-action dried
  yeast
200g white chocolate, chopped
100g pecan nuts, roughly
  chopped
icing sugar, for dusting

1 Lift the bread pan out of the machine and fit the blade. Put the ingredients, except the chocolate and nuts, in the pan, following the order specified in the manual. Add the mashed banana with the milk.

2 Fit the pan into the machine and close the lid. Set to a 750g (1½ lb) loaf size on the fast/rapid bake programme. Add the chocolate and pecans when the machine beeps.

3 At the end of the programme lift the pan out of the machine and shake the bread out on to a wire rack to cool. Serve dusted with icing sugar.

prep + cook time 1–2 hours, depending on machine
makes 1 large loaf

APPLE & GINGER COILS

dough
2 eggs, beaten
175ml milk
2 tablespoons butter, at room
    temperature
½ teaspoon salt
500g strong white bread flour
50g caster sugar
1¼ teaspoons fast-action dried
    yeast

filling
400g cooking apples, peeled
    and cored
1 tablespoon lemon juice
2 tablespoons water
50g caster sugar
125g luxury mixed dried fruit
2 tablespoons ready-chopped
    crystallised ginger

to finish
2 tablespoons caster sugar
4 tablespoons milk
icing sugar, for dusting

1 Lift the bread pan out of the machine and fit the blade. Put the dough ingredients in the pan, following the order specified in the manual. Fit the pan into the machine and close the lid. Set to the dough programme.

2 Meanwhile, make the filling. Dice the apples and place in a small saucepan with the lemon juice, water, sugar and dried fruit. Cover and simmer for 5 minutes until they are just beginning to soften. Remove the lid and cook for 3–5 minutes more until the liquid has evaporated and the apples are tender and the dried fruits are plumped up. Stir in the ginger; leave to cool.

3 At the end of the programme turn the dough out on to a lightly floured surface. Roll it out to a 38 x 30cm rectangle.

4 Spread the apple mixture over the dough to within about 2cm of the edges. Roll it up, starting from one of the longer edges.

5 Cut the dough into 12 thick slices and arrange the pieces, cut sides up, in 3 rows of 4 coils in a greased roasting tin, with a base measurement of 30 x 20cm. Cover loosely with oiled cling film and leave to rise in a warm place for 30 minutes.

6 Bake in a preheated oven, 200°C (400°F), Gas Mark 6, for 20–25 minutes until golden and the central coils sound hollow when tapped. When they are almost ready, make the glaze by heating together the sugar and milk until the sugar has dissolved. Boil for 1 minute, then brush over the hot bread. Dust with the icing sugar.

prep + cook time 1½–2½ hours, depending on machine + shaping and proving time
makes 12 coils

SOURED CREAM & BERRY BREAD

150ml water
150g full-fat crème fraîche
½ teaspoon salt
grated rind of 1 lemon
425g strong white bread flour
3 tablespoons caster sugar
1 teaspoon fast-action dried yeast
100g mixed dried cherries,
    blueberries and cranberries

1 Lift the bread pan out of the machine and fit the blade. Put the ingredients, except the mixed fruit, in the pan, following the order specified in the manual.
2 Fit the pan into the machine and close the lid. Set to a 750g (1½lb) loaf size on the sweet programme (or basic if the machine does not have a sweet setting). Add the dried fruits when the machine beeps.
3 At the end of the programme lift the pan from the machine and shake the bread out on to a wire rack to cool.

prep + cook time 2¾–3½ hours, depending on machine
makes 1 large loaf

PINE NUT, LEMON & CARDAMOM LOAF

dough
20 cardamom pods
finely grated rind and juice of
    2 lemons
about 135ml water (see step 1)
1 large egg, beaten
50g unsalted butter, softened
½ teaspoon salt
3 tablespoons milk powder
425g strong white bread flour
50g caster sugar
1¼ teaspoons fast-action dried
    yeast

to finish
150g pine nuts, toasted
50g flaked almonds
150g sultanas
1 tablespoon lemon juice
65g icing sugar

1 Grind the cardamom pods using a pestle and mortar to extract the seeds. Discard the shells and grind the seeds to break them up. Put the lemon rind and juice in a measuring jug and make it up to 225ml with water.
2 Lift the bread pan out of the machine and fit the blade. Put the dough ingredients in the pan, following the order specified in the manual.
3 Fit the pan into the machine and close the lid. Set to the dough programme.
4 At the end of the programme turn the dough out on to a lightly floured surface and knead in the pine nuts, almonds and sultanas until evenly distributed. Shape the dough into a log shape, about 25cm long, and place it on a large, greased baking sheet. Cover loosely with oiled cling film and leave to rise in a warm place for about 45 minutes or until almost doubled in size.

5 Bake in a preheated oven, 220°C (425°F), Gas Mark 7, for about 25 minutes until risen and golden and the base sounds hollow when tapped. Cool on a wire rack.
6 Beat together the lemon juice and icing sugar to make a thin icing. Drizzle over the bread to decorate.

prep + cook time 1½–2½ hours, depending on machine + shaping and proving time
makes 1 medium loaf

GLOSSARY

balsamic vinegar made from a regional wine of white trebbiano grapes specially processed then aged in antique wooden casks to give the exquisite pungent flavour. It is only authentic when it comes from the province of Modena, Italy.

barley malt extract sweet and treacly, malt extract is made from germinated barley grain. Available from health food shops and online.

bicarbonate of soda also called baking soda; used in baking as a raising agent.

black onion seeds also known as nigella or kalonji seeds; slightly bitter small black seeds, popularly sprinkled on Indian flatbreads.

buttermilk cultured milk with 1.8g fat per 100ml and a slightly sour taste. Low-fat yogurt can be substituted.

candied peel crystallised or glacé citrus peel, available whole (in large slices) or mixed (diced into small cubes).

capers the grey-green buds of a warm climate shrub sold either dried and salted or pickled in vinegar brine.

caraway seeds a member of the parsley family; available in seed or ground form.

cheese
Cheddar the most common cows' milk cheese; should be aged and hard.
feta a crumbly textured goats'- or sheeps'-milk cheese with a sharp, salty taste.
goats' made from goats' milk, goats' cheese has an earthy, strong taste. Can be purchased in both soft and firm textures, in various shapes and sizes, sometimes rolled in ash or herbs. Available from most supermarkets and delicatessens.
Manchego aged Spanish sheeps' milk cheese; creamy cheese with a distinctive piquant flavour.
Parmesan a sharp-tasting, dry, hard cheese, made from skimmed or semi-skimmed milk and aged for at least a year.

clotted cream a thick cream associated with South West England. It is made by heating whole cow's milk and leaving it to cool slowly in shallow pans so that the cream content rises to the surface forming 'clots'.

coriander also known as cilantro or chinese parsley; bright-green-leafed herb with a pungent flavour, also comes as a dried herb. Coriander seeds and ground coriander are also available, they must never be used to replace fresh coriander or vice versa.

cornmeal coarse flour ground from dried corn (maize).

cream of tartar the acid ingredient in baking powder; added to confectionery mixtures to help prevent sugar from crystallising. Keeps frostings creamy and improves volume when beating egg whites.

crème fraîche a mature fermented cream with a slightly tangy flavour and velvety rich texture; similar in thickness to soured cream.

date syrup sweet syrup extracted from dates; used as an alternative sweetener in place of sugar or honey. Available from health food shops and online.

ghee clarified butter; with the milk solids removed, this fat can be heated to a very high cooking temperature without burning.

ginger
crystallised dried ginger root preserved in a sweet sugar coating.
root also called fresh or green ginger; the thick gnarled root of a tropical plant. Can be kept, peeled, covered with dry sherry in a jar and refrigerated, or frozen in an airtight container.

glacé cherries also known as candied cherries; they are boiled in heavy sugar syrup and then dried. Used in cakes, breads and sweets.

milk powder manufactured dairy product made by evaporating milk until it is a dry powder. Used in baking when adding liquid milk would make the result too thin.

mixed spice a blend of ground spices usually consisting of cinnamon, allspice and nutmeg.

molasses thick, dark treacly by-product of sugar refining.

oatmeal made by finely grinding dried oats. Comes in several grades, from super-fine to coarse. Fine and medium grades are best for porridge, oatcakes and cookies while coarser grades can be used as a topping for breads as they hold their shape well.

paprika ground dried pepper; available in sweet, smoked or hot varieties.

pine nuts also known as pignoli; small, cream-coloured kernels obtained from the cones of different varieties of pine trees.

polenta a flour-like cereal made of ground corn; similar to cornmeal but finer and lighter in colour; also the name of the dish made from it.

semolina flour made from the hard part of the wheat; used in making pasta and couscous.

sugar
brown an extremely soft, fine granulated sugar retaining molasses for its deep colour and flavour.
caster also known as superfine or finely granulated table sugar. used mainly in baking.
granulated coarse grained sugar, also known as table sugar.
icing finely milled sugar, also known as confectioners' or powdered sugar.
molasses thick, dark treacly by-product of sugar refining.

vanilla extract obtained from vanilla beans infused in water; a non-alcoholic version of vanilla essence.

wheat germ an edible section of the wheat kernel valued for its rich nutritional content; adds a distinct flavour and texture to baking.

xanthan gum a powder that is used in gluten-free baking to replace the elastic qualities that gluten-free flours lack. It is available from health food stores and some supermarkets.

INDEX

A
apple & ginger coils 118

B
bacon & beer soda bread 50
bananas: white chocolate & banana
    loaf 117
barley flakes: mini barley flower pot
    loaves 72
barley malt extract
    date & malted barley bread 93
    mini barley flower pot loaves 72
basil: buttered garlic & basil
    sticks 27
beer: bacon & beer soda bread 50
brioche: chocolate brioche buns 79
broad beans: goats' cheese & bean
    mini loaves 113
buns
    chocolate brioche 79
    drizzled orange & poppy seed
        75
    hot cross 83
buttered garlic & basil sticks 27
buttermilk: oatmeal & buttermilk
    bread 89

C
cardamom pods: pine nut, lemon &
    cardamom loaf 122
cheddar: yogurt, cheddar & rosemary
    muffins 76
chillies
    chilli & smoked paprika bread 94
    chilli chocolate bread 101
    chilli corn bread 46

chocolate
    chocolate & pecan spiral 62
    chocolate brioche buns 79
    chilli chocolate bread 101
    white chocolate & banana loaf 117
cornmeal: chilli corn bread 46
cottage loaf 16
courgettes: minted courgette & lemon
    loaf 98
couronne 12, 24

D
dates
    date & malted barley bread 93
    date & walnut soda bread 57
decorations 13
dough
    cutting 12
    keeping 12

E
enriching ingredients 7

F
fancy rolls 71
farmhouse white loaf 23
feta: gluten-free feta & herb loaf 38
figs
    fig & walnut bread 54
    gingered fig & orange bread 61
flatbreads, asian-style 106
flours 6–7
focaccia, rosemary & olive oil 28
fruit (dried)
    apple & ginger coils 118
    baby panettones 80

hot cross buns 83
gluten-free spicy fruit & seed
    bread 58
soured cream & berry bread 121
three kings ring 65

G
garlic: buttered garlic & basil sticks 27
garnishes 13
ginger
    apple & ginger coils 118
    gingered fig & orange bread 61
glazes 13
gluten-free bread
    feta & herb loaf 38
    spicy fruit & seed bread 58
goats' cheese & bean mini loaves 113
granary & pumpkin bread 41

H
herbs: gluten-free feta & herb loaf 38
honey: wheat germ & honey loaf 19
hot cross buns 83

L
lemons
    minted courgette & lemon loaf 98
    pine nut, lemon & cardamom
        loaf 122
liquids 7

M
manchego: spinach & manchego ring
    loaf 102
mini barley flower pot loaves 72

minted courgette & lemon loaf 98
mixed seed bread 20
muffins, yogurt, cheddar &
    rosemary 76

N
naan breads, seeded 105

O
oatmeal & buttermilk bread 89
olives
    olive & tomato tear & share
        bread 42
    olive bread 34
olive oil: rosemary & olive oil focaccia
    28
onions
    onion & tomato schiacciata 97
    spiced potato & onion bread 45
oranges
    drizzled orange & poppy seed
        buns 75
    gingered fig & orange bread 61

P
panetonnes, baby 80
paprika: chilli & smoked paprika
    bread 94
parmesan: sage & parmesan flutes 37
pecan nuts: chocolate & pecan spiral
    62
pepper: salt & pepper crusted
    rolls 110
peppers: roasted red pepper &
    rosemary slippers
pine nut, lemon & cardamom loaf 122

pitta bread 31
potatoes: spiced potato & onion
    bread 45
pretzels, salted 12, 109
pumpkin seeds: granary & pumpkin
    bread 41

R
rolls
    fancy 71
    salt & pepper crusted 110
    wholemeal 68
rosemary
    roasted red pepper & rosemary
        slippers 49
    rosemary & olive oil focaccia 28
    yogurt, cheddar & rosemary
        muffins 76
rye flour: fast-baked rye & caraway
    bread 90

S
salt 7
    salt & pepper crusted rolls 110
    salted pretzels 109
schiacciata, onion & tomato 97
sage & parmesan flutes 37
seeds
    drizzled orange & poppy seed
        buns 75
    fast-baked rye & caraway
        bread 90
    gluten-free spicy fruit & seed
        bread 58
    granary & pumpkin bread 41
    mixed seed bread 20

seeded naan breads 105
speedy sesame loaf 86
wheat germ & honey loaf 19
soda bread
    bacon & beer 50
    date & walnut 57
soured cream & berry bread 121
speedy sesame loaf 86
spinach & manchego ring loaf 102
splits, devonshire 114
storing bread 7
sugar 7

T
three kings ring 65
tomatoes
    olive & tomato tear & share
        bread 42
    onion & tomato schiacciata 97

W
walnuts
    date & walnut soda bread 57
    fig & walnut bread 54
wheat germ & honey loaf 19
white loaf, farmhouse 23
wholemeal rolls 68

Y
yeast 7
yogurt, cheddar & rosemary
    muffins 76

CONVERSION CHARTS

measures

One metric tablespoon holds 20ml; one metric teaspoon holds 5ml.

All cup and spoon measurements are level. The most accurate way of measuring dry ingredients is to weigh them. When measuring liquids, use a clear glass or plastic jug with metric markings.

We use large eggs with an average weight of 60g.

dry measures

METRIC	IMPERIAL
15g	½oz
30g	1oz
60g	2oz
90g	3oz
125g	4oz (¼lb)
155g	5oz
185g	6oz
220g	7oz
250g	8oz (½lb)
280g	9oz
315g	10oz
345g	11oz
375g	12oz (¾lb)
410g	13oz
440g	14oz
470g	15oz
500g	16oz (1lb)
750g	24oz (1½lb)
1kg	32oz (2lb)

liquid measures

METRIC	IMPERIAL
30ml	1 fluid oz
60ml	2 fluid oz
100ml	3 fluid oz
125ml	4 fluid oz
150ml	5 fluid oz
190ml	6 fluid oz
250ml	8 fluid oz
300ml	10 fluid oz
500ml	16 fluid oz
600ml	20 fluid oz
1000ml (1 litre)	32 fluid oz

length measures

3mm	⅛in
6mm	¼in
1cm	½in
2cm	¾in
2.5cm	1in
5cm	2in
6cm	2½in
8cm	3in
10cm	4in
13cm	5in
15cm	6in
18cm	7in
20cm	8in
23cm	9in
25cm	10in
28cm	11in
30cm	12in (1ft)

oven temperatures

These are fan-assisted temperatures. If you have a conventional oven (ie. not fan-assisted), increase temperatures by 10–20°.

	°C (CELSIUS)	°F (FAHRENHEIT)	GAS MARK
Very low	100	210	½
Low	130	260	1–2
Moderately low	140	280	3
Moderate	160	325	4–5
Moderately hot	180	350	6
Hot	200	400	7–8
Very hot	220	425	9